Praise for
The B2B Innovator's Map

"When it comes to product leadership, Daniel is the best in the business. I've had the great fortune to work with him and benefited greatly from his thoughts on product innovation. Luckily, he's put that wisdom into the book you're holding in your hands. Needless to say, Daniel's new book will be a constant companion as I build my next enterprise software product."

—**ROB TIFFANY**, Vice President of Strategy at Ericsson

"Building successful technology products for enterprises (B2B) is dramatically different from consumer tech (B2C) products. Much of the popular writing on product strategy, innovation, and scale-up assumes simpler consumer-focused markets where our buyers are also our users; sales cycles are short; problems have a human face, and no single customer dominates our quarter's revenue.

Daniel Elizalde is a twenty-year veteran of enterprise product innovation and market success. In The B2B Innovator's Map, he takes us through the strategies and complexities of understanding the pains and delivering value to not just one customer—who may have unique problems—but our first ten customers. This sets the stage for the growth and massive profitability that our companies need. This is a book that every B2B strategist, product manager, investor, and company founder needs."

—**RICH MIRONOV**, CEO and "smokejumper" CPO

"Fabulous real-world examples from someone who's been there/done that. Daniel Elizalde has created an excellent guide for anyone navigating the treacherous waters of building enterprise software. I wish I had this book ten years ago; it would have saved me from lots of pain!"

—**ERIC SIMONE**, Co-founder and CEO at ClearBlade, Inc.

"Daniel has a unique blend of lean experimentation skills combined with both the worlds of software and hardware. He iterates through complex B2B solutions while speaking in terms that people understand."

—**DAVID BLAND**, co-author of *Testing Business Ideas*

"Daniel brings a pragmatic, step-by-step, real-world-based framework for corralling innovation to not only win over those first ten customers but to put the product development process on the proper trajectory to drive repeatability and scale."

—**BILL SCHMARZO**, author and Customer Advocate at Dell Technologies

"With this book, Daniel Elizalde has crafted a much-needed guide on how to build a B2B business from scratch, which can be a challenging undertaking, but Daniel is a world-class expert on the topic. Future B2B entrepreneurs are lucky to be able to tap into Daniel's expertise and have this book to guide them toward their first ten customers."

—**TENDAYI VIKI**, author of *Pirates In The Navy*.

"A beautifully clear and coherent guide to the murky early days of building enterprise products. Elizalde has done a wonderful job of making his hard-won wisdom available and actionable to the next generation of B2B innovators and product leaders. I very much wish I'd had this book in hand throughout my whole career."

—**ROB FITZPATRICK**, entrepreneur and author of *The Mom Test*

"Daniel's expert insights break the complex and daunting process of B2B innovation into clear, actionable steps. Climatetech startups developing enterprise software will especially appreciate his advice for navigating complex stakeholder dynamics and his framework for investing time and effort where it matters most."

—**KATIE GEUSZ**, Director of Programs at Greentown Labs

"This book is a must-read for anyone working with B2B and innovative enterprise products who wants to accelerate their success. Daniel puts his many years of experience in B2B and innovation into this practical guide, including real-world examples of the innovation journey. In the many years I've known Daniel, this book is by far the strongest example of his expertise made available for the world to consume."

—**CESAR GAMEZ**, Vice President of Systems Research and Development for NI

"In today's fast-paced world of software product innovation, where everything is possible and 'starchitects' hold sway, it is so easy to disregard even core tenets of innovation discipline as impractical or assumed. And yet, how much time are we spending revisiting the fundamentals on products we are pushing to scale? This book is a fast, fun, and highly referenceable reminder that experience cannot possibly replace good strategy in early product design."

—**MIGUEL MORALES**, IoT Sales and Product Lead at Microsoft

"Daniel is a good friend and fantastic advisor on building products for B2B businesses. I had the great fortune to leverage his skills through a consulting project where the business benefited from his ideas on product development. The book is a great way to leverage all his experience and insights for anyone who wants to build world-class B2B products!"

—**VISHWESH (VISH) PAI**, Senior Director of Product Management at ServiceNow

"In The B2B Innovator's Map, Daniel provides a wonderfully simple and easy-to-follow guide for launching new enterprise software products. If you follow the steps described in this book, you will understand the process needed to achieve the success you envisioned when you started your journey. Daniel not only teaches the correct steps, but he also identifies the pitfalls you need to stay away from, along with examples of each."

—**WAYNE IRWIN**, Vice President of Operations at Ericsson

"The best lessons and insights come from people who have been in the trenches, led from the front, and have battle scars to show. Daniel Elizalde has over two decades of learnings from the school of hard knocks. In The B2B Innovator's Map, he distills those experiences in easy, bite-size chunks of actionable steps that are extremely beneficial for any B2B entrepreneur, leader, and practitioner. How do you take a vision and convert it into a meaningful product that delivers incredible value to end-users? What steps must you take to drive an innovative idea into a reality that someone will be willing to pay for? The B2B Innovator's Map provides you with a clear path to discover the answers."

—**NEERAJ MATHUR**, Founder and CEO of SavingsOak

The B2B Innovator's Map

The B2B Innovator's Map

How to Get from Idea to Your First Ten Customers

Daniel Elizalde

COPYRIGHT © 2022 DANIEL ELIZALDE

All rights reserved.

THE B2B INNOVATOR'S MAP
How to Get from Idea to Your First Ten Customers

ISBN	978-1-5445-2928-8	*Hardcover*
	978-1-5445-2927-1	*Paperback*
	978-1-5445-2926-4	*Ebook*

Contents

Introduction 1

1. Mapping the Innovation Journey 9

2. Strategic Alignment 35

3. Market Discovery 63

4. User Discovery 111

5. Solution Planning 147

6. Prototyping 169

7. Early Adopter 215

8. The Next Stage in Your Innovation Journey 251

Acknowledgments 259

About the Author 263

To Megan,
Your love and support make everything possible.

To Maya,
Mi niña preciosa.

Introduction

THROUGHOUT THE YEARS, I'VE TALKED TO HUNDREDS OF innovators. Although every situation is different, our conversations tend to be very similar: they start full of optimism as they tell me about their purpose, their ideas, and how they plan to impact the world. I love that part of the conversation. But then, invariably, the optimism takes a back seat to the anxiety and frustration coming from an inevitable part of innovation: uncertainty.

Innovation, by definition, is uncertain. You are creating something completely new, and there is no way to know if your product will succeed in the market. Uncertainty can cause you to second-guess every move and wonder if you are making the right decisions. Uncertainty can also make you question if you have what it takes to pull this off.

Many innovators try to reduce uncertainty by reading everything they can get their hands on. I remember talking with a startup CEO whose office was covered in business books. He had books on shelves. Books on the floor. And more books on his desk that were barely visible under piles of reports and printed blog posts. "The problem," he told me, "is that each of these books covers a small portion of the innovation journey, but it's hard to know where you are or which tools work best for each situation. Plus, most innovation, product, and strategy books," he continued, "are designed for Business-to-Consumer (B2C) products and not Business-to-Business (B2B) or Enterprise products." He said, "I'm tired of reading about approaches that have nothing to do with my industry or my type of product. I'm telling you, Daniel, if I hear advice about driving traffic to an A/B test one more time, I'm going to flip!"

Does this sound familiar? Well, you are not alone.

I've heard variations of this conversation many times, and I'm sure you have too. For me, these conversations hit very close to home. I've worked on many B2B products throughout my career, and I've always felt like an outlier. It is difficult to find the right direction or the correct techniques that work in a B2B context. That is why I wrote this book.

I wrote this book for *you*, the innovator responsible for launching new B2B digital products to market. This book is a practical guide to tame uncertainty throughout the innovation journey. By the end of this book, you'll have a turn-by-turn map to navigate the innovation journey so that you always know where you are and what your next step should be. You'll have the tools and techniques for reducing the uncertainty of

Introduction

understanding your market and the needs of your customers. Plus, you'll get all the tools you need to reduce the uncertainty on whether your potential solution can solve your customers' needs. I will also show you how to work with your internal stakeholders to ensure you retain their support throughout the innovation journey. No more doubting or second-guessing your decisions.

In short, this book is about clarity. But it is also about focus and setting concrete milestones.

The only way to reduce uncertainty is to define those concrete milestones and create a plan to get there. But unfortunately, most companies focus on abstract goals such as "getting to product-market fit" or "getting to scale." The problem with these goals is they are not actionable and, therefore, not attainable. Ask five people to define product-market fit, and you'll get five different definitions. In this book, I avoid abstract targets and give you a map to get from idea to your first ten customers. It doesn't get more concrete than that!

You might be wondering, *Why focus only on your first ten customers?* The ultimate goal of any new product is to go from idea to scale, but the reality is that most new enterprise software products fail before reaching their first ten customers. Let that sink in for a moment.

The key to success is delivering value to the first ten companies that purchase your product and using that as concrete evidence of market traction so that you can plan your next step. And let's be honest, if you can't deliver value to your first ten customers, how do you expect to scale to your next 100 or 1,000?

Before I introduce you to the six stages of the B2B Innovator's Map that get you from idea to your first ten customers, I want to define a few terms I use throughout the book: "innovator," "enterprise software," and "customer."

The term "innovator" often brings images of the greatest minds in history, such as Albert Einstein, Marie Curie, Thomas Edison, Nikola Tesla, and Elon Musk. Although these people are indeed innovators, that's not at all what this book is about. In this book, I use the term innovator to describe the person (or team) responsible for bringing a new digital product to market. Your title might vary anywhere from founder, CEO, or leader in product management, design, technology, marketing, business development, strategy, finance, etc. But title aside, if you are responsible (or involved) in bringing new digital products to market, then congratulations, you are an innovator! And therefore, this book is for you.

Now, what do I mean by "enterprise software"? Enterprise software is an umbrella term for many different types of applications that solve the pains of an organization—as opposed to a single person. By definition, enterprise software uses a Business-to-Business model (B2B) instead of a Business-to-Consumer model (B2C). In this book, I use

Introduction

enterprise software, B2B product, digital product, and B2B solution interchangeably.

Some B2B solutions support organization-wide processes, such as email or other communication tools managed by the information technology (IT) department. Others support the business processes of a particular department, including customer relationship management (CRM) solutions for sales, lead generation tools for marketing, people management and recruiting solutions for HR, etc. I also use the term enterprise software for more specialized types of applications, such as electronic medical records systems in healthcare, eCommerce and payment solutions for retail, logistics solutions for supply chain, monitoring solutions for manufacturing, control solutions for the energy industry, network management tools, and any other operational technology (OT) applications out there.

Grouping so many characteristics under the umbrella of enterprise software might seem counterproductive for a book about innovation and strategy, but all B2B software applications share characteristics. These include the complexity of dealing with buyers and a large ecosystem of users, the need to iterate and test assumptions, the importance of internal alignment with your leadership team, and the difficulty of working through pilot programs. Understanding these characteristics can help you build successful enterprise software, regardless of your industry, market category, or customer size.

The last term I want to define is "customer." In a B2B context, a customer is a company, not a user. Delivering value to your first ten customers means building a product that solves the needs of ten different companies. Each of your first ten customers might have dozens, or even hundreds, of users.

Over 20 years, I have managed the lifecycle of complex enterprise software and industrial Internet of Things (IoT) products in many industries, including renewable energy, eCommerce, manufacturing, telecommunications, and automotive. I have served in several leadership positions, such as V.P., Head of IoT at Ericsson, and Head of Products at Stem (an AI-powered energy storage company in Silicon Valley). I have also helped organizations drive enterprise software from idea to commercialization, both as an Innovation and Product Leadership Coach and as an Instructor at Stanford University.

Building on my experience helping over 1,500 product professionals, this book gives you a step-by-step framework to navigate the early stages of the innovation journey. I call this framework the B2B Innovator's Map, and it includes these six stages:

1. Strategic Alignment

2. Market Discovery

3. User Discovery

4. Solution Planning

Introduction

5. Prototyping

6. Early Adopter

To illustrate the book's concepts, tools, and techniques, I've included many real-world stories I've experienced throughout my career. In most stories, I've changed the names of the companies, people, industries, and applications to protect the identity of those involved.

The lessons included in this book are not theoretical. They come from years of doing the work. You can be confident that each lesson has been tested in the field and has helped startups and large corporations like yours advance their innovation journey.

B2B product innovation is a huge topic. As I wrote this book, it was difficult to decide what to leave in and what to leave out. I decided to be laser-focused on the innovation journey and, therefore, decided to cut out other important areas. But, don't worry, I have you covered. I'm keeping the conversation going on my website, where you can find articles, podcast interviews, and many additional tools, including the companion workbook for this book. You can access all that content and get in touch with me at https://danielelizalde.com.

Thank you so much for reading my book. I hope you find it useful in your innovation journey, and I look forward to seeing your successful product in the market.

Let's get started!

Mapping the Innovation Journey

EARLY IN MY CAREER, I BUILT A GREAT PRODUCT THAT HAD NO future in the market.

One of our biggest customers was a semiconductor company that had purchased several of our automated systems to test the functionality of their microcontrollers in the lab. The customer was pleased with our systems because they could easily create and execute new tests. But after using the system for some time, they realized they struggled to track all the tests they had created. My company wanted to explore if there was an opportunity for a new product here, so they assigned me to look into it. Little did I know I was in for a wild ride.

After several customer interactions, I pitched my leadership team the idea of developing a new application for managing the tests. They thought it was an excellent opportunity, so they gave me the green light to build this new product.

I wanted to be customer-driven, so I worked closely with our customer to define a solution that'd meet their needs. Finally, after a year of development, we deployed version one of our application. The product worked great, and our customer was delighted. This was a real success story. Or so I thought.

Enterprise software is not about solving one person's—or even one organization's—pain. Though we worked closely with *one* company, we didn't validate if other companies had the same pain and if our solution would help them. When our sales team offered the product to other potential customers, the feedback was brutal. For some prospects, the solution was very niche and didn't fit their needs. For others, that particular problem was not big enough to warrant an investment, or they were happy with their current solution. And yet others were not happy with their current solution, but the expense of migrating to a new solution was not worth the trouble.

Soon I realized the hard truth. There wouldn't be a second customer.

Looking back at this story, it is very easy to see why my product failed. At the time, I didn't have the necessary tools to understand the innovation journey, and therefore, I skipped several important steps. We thought we had built a hit product, but the reality is that we failed to do the work of understanding our customers and our target market.

If the prospect of building a failed product scares you, you are not alone. But don't worry. Throughout this book, I'll be by your side every step of the way to make sure this doesn't happen to you. Before we begin mapping the innovation journey, I want to define what I mean by product innovation and the particular challenges you will face when building B2B digital products.

WHAT IS PRODUCT INNOVATION?

Product innovation is the process of creating new products that generate increased value for your customers and your company.

It's not a destination but a journey with many twists and turns. Unfortunately, companies big and small waste a lot of time and money creating software products that don't provide value to customers and, therefore, that nobody wants to buy. These failures are rarely about technology, people, funding, or partnerships. Instead, these failures result from a lack of customer-centricity.

A successful product needs to solve a pain that customers are willing to pay for while at the same time generating a significant return on investment. But many B2B companies short-circuit the innovation journey either because they believe they already know what the market wants or because they don't have the skills and processes to be customer-centric throughout the development process.

In the next sections, I'll walk you through the foundation for becoming customer-centric in the context of B2B, including how to:

1. Understand enterprise customers

2. Map the innovation journey

3. Put it all together

UNDERSTAND ENTERPRISE CUSTOMERS

For Business-to-Consumer (B2C) products, the "customer" is simultaneously the person with the pain, the person who buys the product, and the person who uses it to solve their needs. Therefore, learning the needs of B2C customers is a relatively straightforward effort, since you only need to understand the needs of that one user.

Understanding enterprise customers is very hard. In fact, from my enterprise experience and from coaching dozens of product teams, I can definitively say that understanding enterprise customers is the number one challenge facing B2B innovation teams.

Understanding your enterprise customers means understanding their desired business outcome, as well as the people, processes, and tools involved in achieving that outcome.

Mapping the Innovation Journey

The first step in understanding your enterprise customers is identifying the three categories of people involved in achieving a business outcome:

1. **Champion:** person accountable for achieving a business outcome.

2. **Users:** people internal or external to your customer's organization who use your product as a tool to support the Champion's business outcome.

3. **Buying Committee:** people involved in evaluating and purchasing your product (e.g., the Champion, finance, IT, procurement, partners).

Enterprise sales and marketing teams use multiple names to refer to your customer's business leader, the one who is accountable for achieving a business outcome. Some familiar names include Buyer, Executive Sponsor, Decision-Maker, and Champion. I prefer the term Champion because, in the early stages of the innovation journey, you need more than a Buyer or a Decision-Maker. You require somebody who will partner with you to champion your untested product, someone who will take a leap of faith that your application can solve their problem.

Although this person has the pain you could potentially solve, they might not be the ultimate decision-maker or might not have direct access to a budget to purchase your solution. Instead, the Champion knows how to navigate their organization, and they can get the support they need to bring your solution in-house.

Let's look at an example that shows the complexity of understanding enterprise customers.

The Chief Operating Officer (COO) of a mid-size company is tasked with reducing the company's travel expenses by 30 percent. As part of her initiative to achieve this business outcome, she decides to purchase an enterprise expense tracking solution. Achieving the business outcome will depend on many users across the organization using this expense tracking solution. Let's break down all the people involved in our three categories:

Champion:

- **COO:** responsible for the business outcome of reducing travel expenses by 30 percent.

Users:

- **COO:** serves as both the Champion *and* a user of the solution.

- **Employees:** track expenses and reimbursements.

- **HR manager:** sets travel policies in the system.

- **Line managers:** approve expense reports.

- **Directors and VPs:** get roll-up reports of expenses for their area.

- **Assistants:** manage approvals and expense tracking for senior executives.

- **IT manager:** controls access and security.

- **System integrator:** develops integrations to other enterprise solutions.

Buying Committee:

- **VP of IT:** possesses budget and purchasing authority (i.e., buyer).

- **Director of Compliance:** reviews and approves service-level agreements (SLAs) and any other legal documents involved in purchasing the software.

- **COO:** acts as the Champion, a user, and part of the buying committee.

This example makes it easy to grasp the complexity of building enterprise software products. **For your product to be successful, it needs to provide an effective way to support the workflows of all users, and all these workflows need to work together to support the desired business outcome of your Champion.**

Enterprise software is complex because you have to balance the needs of your Champion, Users, and Buying Committee while maintaining internal alignment with your organization. Keeping all these pieces working together can feel like a balancing act, so you need a map to navigate the innovation journey. This map should help you leverage your company's strategy, methodically gather insights from your customers, iterate on building a solution, and get sustained support from within your organization.

Let's look in more detail at the six stages of the B2B Innovator's Map to take your product from idea to your first ten customers.

A MAP OF THE INNOVATION JOURNEY

For many companies, focusing on the innovation journey from idea to your first ten customers might sound like a tiny goal. But the reality is that most enterprise software products never get a single customer, let alone ten. If you can deliver value to your first ten customers, then you'll be in a great position to move beyond the innovation journey towards scale.

To help you navigate the innovation journey from idea to your first ten customers, the B2B Innovator's Map is organized into six distinct stages:

Mapping the Innovation Journey

1. Strategic Alignment

2. Market Discovery

3. User Discovery

4. Solution Planning

5. Prototyping

6. Early Adopter

Some stages focus on getting customer insights while other stages focus on getting internal alignment within your company. **Both areas are critical because to drive innovation, you need strong customer evidence *and* solid support from your organization.**

The diagram below shows the six stages of the B2B Innovator's Map, along with the criteria you need to meet to move between stages.

THE B2B INNOVATOR'S MAP

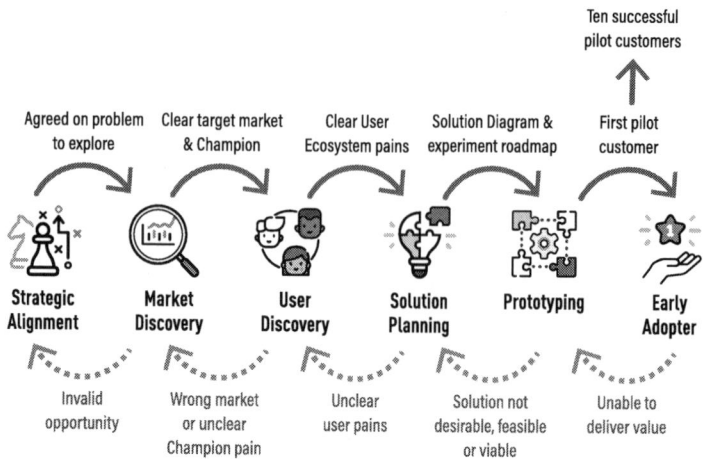

Notice that you can move both forward and backward on the journey, depending on the customer evidence you gathered in that stage. Expect to iterate, moving back and forth between stages, as you gather more customer evidence or realize that your assumptions were correct or incorrect.

For example, in the Strategic Alignment stage, your company might agree to explore a specific customer business outcome. But as you enter the Market Discovery stage and research potential markets for your product, you might discover that your customer's pain in that market is not big enough to support a business.

In that case, you shouldn't proceed to the User Discovery stage, because you already know your customer's pains are not big enough. Instead, you might stay in the Market

Discovery stage, looking for other markets to go after. Or you might go back to the Strategic Alignment stage and agree with your company on a different customer business outcome to explore.

With every iteration, you might advance one stage or move back one or more stages. And that's OK. This method ensures you always focus on the most promising ideas and spend the least amount of effort and resources on ideas that will go nowhere. I know it is scary to talk to your leadership team about "moving backward." But believe me, all successful products go through this flow. By taking a step back when your assumptions are incorrect, you won't be slowing down. Instead, you'll be gaining momentum and saving your company time and money by not chasing a rabbit hole that leads to failed products.

Going from idea to your first ten customers will take time and resources. Maybe you've heard stories about companies that run 100 experiments per week or teams that go from idea to prototype testing in a couple of days. I don't doubt those stories are true, but they most likely come from the B2C world.

Enterprise solutions have different constraints and take much longer, so it is essential to set the right expectation with your stakeholders. For example, just getting access to the right people to interview might take several weeks. But the learnings you'll get outweigh the risk and cost of using the same few weeks to build software based on "gut feel."

THE B2B INNOVATOR'S MAP

Setting this expectation requires ongoing education and alignment across your company. The thought of spending weeks or months just testing an idea might be difficult to grasp for many people in your organization. You'll get a lot of pushback from executives directing you to just "do something quickly," to get this "innovation process" out of the way so that you can start building the actual product.

> **PRO TIP:** The six stages of the B2B Innovator's Map are an accelerator, not an obstacle. They will help you reduce risk, making it more likely that your product will find traction. Skipping any of these stages will result in an incomplete understanding of your customer, which results in poor product decisions. That road leads to products nobody wants, so don't fall into that trap.

Below is a summary of the six stages. At every stage, you'll learn something new about your customer, and you'll continue to fine-tune your offering until you can deliver value to your first ten customers. In the following chapters, I deep-dive into each of these stages, arming you with all the frameworks, tools, and techniques you need to drive your new product forward.

1. Strategic Alignment

In the Strategic Alignment stage, you'll learn techniques for collaborating with your leadership team to effectively explore opportunities aligned with your company's strategy and to agree on a particular customer's business outcome to explore. Examples of business outcomes include helping your customer reduce their travel expenses, lowering their electricity bill, and tracking assets more efficiently.

Along with that agreement, you'll define success metrics, secure resources, define your innovation team and Advisory Board, and agree on how to report progress throughout your innovation journey.

2. Market Discovery

In the Market Discovery stage, you will explore the market opportunity for the customer's business outcome you agreed to during the Strategic Alignment stage. You'll learn techniques for narrowing down to a specific *target market* to go after, including industry, company size, geography, and use case.

In the Market Discovery stage, you'll also research whether the target market you selected is big enough to support your new business. You'll then spend time understanding the characteristics and pains of your Champion.

Selecting a target market does not guarantee you'll find traction for your product; it only means you have narrowed down your universe of options. To understand if your idea has potential or not, you need to deep-dive into the challenges of your customer in this market. For example, you might discover that the pain in that market is not big enough to demand a new solution or that there aren't enough companies experiencing the pain to support your business. At that point, you can agree with your company to look into a different market or go back to the Strategic Alignment stage to agree on another customer's business outcome to explore.

3. User Discovery

You selected a target market and identified your customer's pain in the Market Discovery stage. This information is critical for defining a product roadmap, but it is not enough. Now you need to understand the pains and workflows of all the people within your customer's organization who will use your solution and whose collective output will resolve the Champion's pain. I call all these different users your *User Ecosystem*.

In the User Discovery stage, you will learn a framework to identify, research, and prioritize your User Ecosystem throughout the enterprise customer journey, from sales to installation, deployment, operations, and more.

4. Solution Planning

Stages one, two, and three of the journey focus on understanding the problem to solve, the market, and the people who experience that problem. Stages four, five, and six focus on incrementally testing and developing your solution to address that problem.

The goal of the Solution Planning stage is to plan for the work ahead. This is the time to discuss how you and your team will approach testing and building a solution to solve your Champion's pain.

By planning, I don't mean the Waterfall way of planning. Instead, during this stage, you will:

- prioritize the users to focus on first;

- create a Solution Diagram to get alignment on what you plan to build; and

- create an experiment roadmap to test with your prospects during the Prototyping stage and to test with your first ten pilot customers during the Early Adopter stage.

This stage also helps you align with your leadership team on your next steps and agree on the support you will need moving forward, including people, funds, equipment, and vendors.

5. Prototyping

The Prototyping stage focuses on building prototypes to test with prospects in your target market. In other words, it's about experimenting and getting real-world evidence on whether your solution can solve your customer's pain.

With every experiment you make, you'll gain new customer insights to incorporate into a new iteration of your solution. These insights allow your solution to move from sketches to low-fidelity prototypes to high-fidelity prototypes until you finally get your first paid customer and deliver a working prototype.

Experimentation applies to every component in your offering, including your technical solution, monetization model, services, and partnerships. In the Prototyping stage, you'll learn tools and techniques to test your assumptions across three dimensions:

- **Desirability:** does your target market want your offering?

- **Viability:** can you make money with your offering?

- **Feasibility:** can your company build and operate the resulting solution?

6. Early Adopter

Getting your first paid customer is a huge milestone. It means that at least one Champion sees your solution's potential, and they believe you can provide value. But you haven't demonstrated that value yet. In the Early Adopter stage, you'll work closely with your first ten customers to ensure you can deliver value.

Your goals during the Early Adopter stage are:

- Demonstrate (in the field) that your solution can solve your customer's pain.

- Continue testing for desirability, feasibility, and viability as you learn what it takes to deploy and operate your product.

During this stage, you'll put together all the tools, skills, and insights you've gathered from previous stages and work closely with your first pilot customers to deliver value. You will also start testing your assumptions throughout the enterprise customer journey and fine-tuning your product's features to deliver on your promise.

The learnings you'll get from your first customer will be invaluable, but they are not enough for you to know if your offering has potential in your target market. To get more confidence that you genuinely know your customers and that you can solve their problems, you need to deliver the same value to ten customers.

Your role as an innovator is to reduce the risk of launching new products into the market. Therefore, to manage that risk, you must focus on concrete milestones you can measure, such as providing value to your first ten customers. Abstract milestones, like product-market fit, are not useful because they're subjective. It is very difficult to plan, measure, and execute towards a product-market fit milestone.

On the other hand, setting a concrete milestone, such as providing value to your first ten customers, enables you to communicate a clear picture of the innovation journey to the rest of your organization. With a clear goal in mind, now everybody can understand what the goal is and how much progress you are making toward it.

Furthermore, in the world of enterprise software, every customer can be very different from each other, even if they belong to the same target market. For example, your enterprise customers might have different organizational structures, legacy systems to integrate with, distinct compliance requirements, etc.

By the time you deliver your tenth pilot project, you will feel confident that you've seen most of the variations you will encounter in that market. You'll start seeing the same patterns and the same type of challenges from your Champions and User Ecosystem.

Delivering value to your first ten customers doesn't mean you are ready to scale. It only means that you have an excellent understanding of your customer, and you know you can deliver value to this target market. Ten customers serve as a concrete milestone to start discussions with your leadership team on what the next step for your new product should be. Making these decisions before delivering value to ten customers is premature and often leads to failure.

PUT IT ALL TOGETHER

To illustrate how the six stages of the B2B Innovator's Map work together, let me expand on the example I mentioned earlier about managing travel expenses.

Julie was a director of technology for a company developing accounting software for mid-to-large corporations. Her leadership team wanted to expand their product portfolio, so they assigned Julie to lead this innovation effort. Julie had been here before. In the past, the company invested heavily in several initiatives that went nowhere. Those projects were based on internal assumptions, and their focus was to build something fast to beat the competition. Julie knew she had to do things differently, so she worked with her team to guide her company from their idea to their first ten customers.

During the **Strategic Alignment** stage, Julie worked with her leadership team to agree on the business outcome they wanted to solve for their customers. Based on market data and other insights, Julie's leadership team believed there was an opportunity to expand their portfolio into the "expense tracking" business. Although this wasn't very specific, it was enough for Julie to move to the Market Discovery stage and start exploring the pains around expense tracking and who could benefit from such a solution.

During the **Market Discovery** stage, Julie and her team worked to identify the target market they should go after. Her leadership team had a hunch that large corporations have more expenses to track and would, therefore, be excellent targets for a new product. Julie talked to several people in Fortune 500 companies who could be potential targets (i.e., her Champions). She discovered that, although these people had pain around expenses, they already had enterprise systems to handle their needs. In all her conversations, she couldn't find a real opportunity for a new product.

Julie went back to the drawing board and, after more research, discovered that smaller companies didn't have expense tracking systems. Therefore, they would be a better target. Julie talked to several people in these smaller companies and verified there was an opportunity there. She learned that her Champion is usually the COO tasked with reducing company expenses. She also discovered that, from all possible expenses to track, travel expenses were the most troublesome ones. Now, Julie had good evidence of a potential target market, potential Champions, and a few specific pains to solve. Julie had to convince her leadership team that the opportunity was with smaller companies and not with large corporations. Since she had objective customer evidence, she was able to make her case. Now, with her leadership team behind her, Julie moved forward to the User Discovery stage.

During the **User Discovery** stage, Julie and her team talked to Champions from many small companies to understand who else would be involved in the process of tracking travel expenses. Julie learned there were three categories of users: expense report creators, approvers, and system administrators. Julie scheduled interviews with people from all of these groups, and she was able to get a clear picture of the many workflows that her product would need to support. With this information, Julie was ready to advance to the Solution Planning stage.

During the **Solution Planning** stage, Julie and her team sketched out the various components their application would need to support all the customer workflows she identified. While defining their Solution Diagram, her team noticed some significant gaps in their user understanding, so they decided to go back to the User Discovery stage for a couple of weeks to gather the missing info.

Once the Solution Diagram was complete, they realized their solution needed to support many users and many scenarios. The next step was to prioritize where to begin. Julie decided to narrow the scope. During her conversations with Champions from multiple companies, she learned that the most critical travel expenses to track were from the sales team, so she decided to focus on solving for the sales team first, which limited the scope to just a couple of user types and a couple of workflows. That scope was enough to test out whether their solution could deliver value to their customers.

During the **Prototyping** stage, Julie and her team tested their proposed solution by showing their Champion and potential users click-through prototypes. She also used these prototypes to showcase her progress internally, enabling her leadership team to visualize what this product could be. Julie's team iterated through many prototypes, incorporating customer feedback, keeping the ideas that worked, and discarding those that didn't.

As the team gathered more evidence that their solution was gaining traction, they moved on from click-through prototypes and started building their prototypes in actual software. With every customer feedback iteration, their software gained functionality, and at some point, it was robust enough that one Champion offered to buy it. Julie had secured their first pilot customer! With this early win, Julie secured the backing of her leadership team to move into the Early Adopter stage.

During the **Early Adopter** stage, Julie's team deployed their solution for the first time and worked tirelessly to ensure their product delivered the value it promised to their Champion. At the same time, Julie worked with her Business Development team to secure additional pilot customers.

Mapping the Innovation Journey

After a few months, Julie and her team had confirmed ten pilot customers, and they had iterated enough on the early issues that they were consistently delivering value to all their customers. Julie had taken her company from idea to their first ten successful customers! In the process, she had saved the company a lot of time and money because she minimized the risk of building a product nobody wanted. Thanks to all of her efforts, Julie opened a new line of revenue for the company and gained the trust of her leadership team to continue investing in new products. Julie continued leading all new product initiatives, now in her new role as Vice President of Product Innovation.

I wrote this story to illustrate a "happy path" where Julie's journey is almost seamless across the innovation journey. But as you know, a "happy path" doesn't exist in the real world. As you start your own innovation journey, keep in mind that you'll need to make many course corrections and iterate multiple times on each of these stages. Also, know that most companies never make it to the Early Adopter or even the Prototyping stage. But even if your company only makes it to the first stage (Strategic Alignment) and decides to abandon your project, that is still a big win!

Most companies skip all these stages and try to go from idea to scale, often resulting in time and money wasted. If you can gather real-world insights and quickly iterate between stages, you'll not only be saving your company time and money, but you'll also be increasing your chances of success.

In Julie's story, I only focused on the flow and the outputs of each of the stages. So if you feel like you are missing the "how" in this story, don't worry. I have you covered. In the following chapters, I'll give you a deep dive into each stage and share with you all the tools, frameworks, and techniques you need to succeed.

DOWNLOAD THE COMPANION B2B INNOVATOR'S KIT

I wrote this book as a practical, hands-on guide. You'll get the most value if you work with your team to apply all the concepts to your own innovation journey. To help you, I created a companion kit that includes:

- The companion B2B Innovator's Workbook with all the relevant questions you and your team need to answer as you go through the innovation journey.

- Additional resources to support you through your journey.

The B2B Innovator's Kit is my way of saying thank you for buying my book. You can download your kit for free at https://danielelizalde.com/b2b-innovators-kit/

I recommend you download the workbook now and keep it handy as you read the book. That way, you can start filling it out as you go. Most likely, you won't have the answer to all of the workbook's questions right away. And that's normal. Whichever sections you can't answer today should be the sections you focus on first with your team.

By writing this book, I'm hoping my experience catches you at a point in your journey where you can use these learnings to identify shortcomings in your current strategy and navigate the innovation journey toward a successful, customer-centric product. I'm rooting for you!

Strategic Alignment

I ONCE ADVISED A COMPANY WORKING ON A NEW DIGITAL payment solution. My first step was to interview each stakeholder to understand their perspective on the product direction, strategy, and potential challenges ahead. The CEO stated that the new product's goal was to make it easy for their customers to add payment capabilities to mobile apps. The Director of Operations said that the value of this new product was to enable their customers to accept payment in foreign currencies. And the CTO said their customers' main problem was cybersecurity, so the new product was all about encryption and tracking potential fraud.

These three customer business outcomes (mobile payments, payment in foreign currencies, and tracking fraud) are all great opportunities to pursue. The problem is that the product required to solve each of these business outcomes is very different, not to mention that the end-customer that needs each of these products is different as well. The root of the problem was that the company's stakeholders didn't have

Strategic Alignment. They all agreed they needed a new product, but they didn't agree on what problem the product should solve for their customers.

Without internal alignment regarding which customer business outcome to focus on, you can't move forward building your new product. That's why the first stage of the B2B Innovator's Map focuses on getting Strategic Alignment on why you need a new product and what pain(s) this new product should solve for your customers.

On the innovation journey from idea to your first ten customers, you are here:

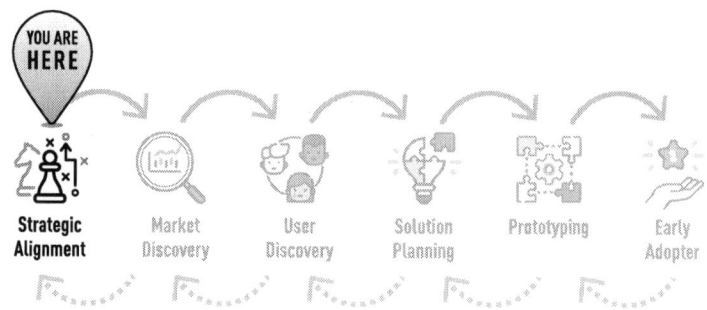

At the beginning of any new initiative, everything is rosy. There's enthusiasm, and it is easy to get everybody on board with the promise of a successful new product. Later, it is guaranteed that you will start running into the inevitable challenges of bringing new software products to market. **If your initiative is not aligned with your company's strategy,**

Strategic Alignment

it'll quickly lose relevance, resources, and executive sponsorship to the next shiny object that comes around.

The trigger for investing in a new product could come from many areas, including:

- A key customer expresses a need, and that's enough to launch into new product development.

- Engineering creates a new piece of technology, and there's a push to bring it to market.

- A competitor releases a new product, creating the need to develop a response to stay relevant.

- There is a shift in the market (due to regulation, pandemics, new technologies, world events, etc.), causing companies to revisit their current strategy.

These triggers can be a good catalyst for innovation, but only if they are backed by a solid innovation strategy. Before developing a new product in response to these triggers, it is crucial to:

1. Define the customer's business outcome.

2. Get agreement on a customer business outcome.

3. Assemble your innovation team.

4. Create an Advisory Board.

5. Agree on progress metrics.

You will then have a clear direction for your innovation initiative, and you will be more likely to arrive at a product that solves a customer need—one your company is willing to invest in.

DEFINE THE CUSTOMER'S BUSINESS OUTCOME

Earlier in my career, I made the mistake of relying 100 percent on the executive team to articulate the pain our new product should solve for our future customers.

Executive teams speak a very different language from product and innovation teams. When asked for clarification, some executives pointed me to a 1,000-slide deck created by consultants based on the overall company strategy. That was informative (sometimes) but useless for what I needed because it was not actionable. Other executives pointed me to generic umbrella statements like, "We need to grow revenue" or "We need to make sure we stay ahead of the competition." Some executives who had just returned from the latest trade show would tell me that we needed an Artificial Intelligence strategy, an IoT strategy, or a cloud strategy—which means nothing at all.

When starting a new product initiative, the direction you are most likely to get from your executive team is around an internal business outcome, such as "increasing revenue" or

Strategic Alignment

"driving revenue from new channels." These outcomes are often anchored on the triggers I mentioned above, and therefore, they are inward-facing as opposed to market-facing. The key here is that, although those are important outcomes, they don't give your team enough information to create a new product and launch it to the market.

The lesson for me was that I shouldn't expect to get the desired customer outcome, precisely in the format I needed it, from my leadership team. On the contrary, it was my responsibility to understand my company's desired outcomes, present product options to meet those goals, receive feedback, and refine my proposal until everybody agreed on how to move forward.

If you are responsible for driving a new product forward, you need to take responsibility for compiling that information and getting buy-in from your leadership team. Your goal before launching any innovation initiative is to gain clarity and agreement on *what* customer problem the company wants to solve and *the timeline* to solve it.

Understanding the desired timeline sets the context for further discussions on what customer problem you could solve in that timeline. I like using McKinsey & Company's Three Horizons of Growth framework[1] to agree on the innovation timeline my company is looking for. McKinsey's

---

1 https://www.mckinsey.com/business-functions/strategy-and-corporate-finance/our-insights/enduring-ideas-the-three-horizons-of-growth

framework defines three different time horizons for bringing a new product to market:

1. Horizon one refers to short-term improvements to existing products. This is the area where most established product and development organizations focus their time.

2. Horizon two refers to a mid-term timeline for launching a new product. Most innovation teams operate on a horizon two mindset, meaning their focus is to generate new products that will generate profits in the midterm. Companies should not expect immediate returns from any initiatives in horizon two.

3. Horizon three refers to research or disruptive innovation. This means that companies working on horizon three projects will not have a product in the market for a long, long time. Companies working on horizon three are in it for the long run and know they need to continue investing in these initiatives for a while before seeing any return.

Getting alignment on which horizon to focus on is a crucial part of the Strategic Alignment stage. If your company's goal is to generate new revenue in the short term (horizon one), then the focus might not be on a new product; instead, you should focus on new features to enhance *existing* products. If the goal is to get new revenue in the midterm (horizon two),

Strategic Alignment

then working on a new product makes sense. And if the goal of the innovation is focused on long-term research (horizon three), then you shouldn't expect to have a product for a long, long time. The concepts of this book apply to horizon two and can be reused for new features in horizon one.

I wish there was a magic formula to get Strategic Alignment across your organization, but there is not. The only way is to work closely with your leadership team to define and agree on the customer business outcome to explore and the timeline to explore it.

I want to emphasize two words from that statement: **explore** and **agree**.

You need to set the expectation that innovation is about *exploring* a new area to understand the market and customer opportunity. You might discover a big opportunity, but you might not. You also need to *agree* with your executive team that *this* particular business outcome is something the company is willing to invest in.

In summary, this agreement is critical because it

- ensures the problem space you'll pursue is aligned with the overall company strategy;

- ensures you'll continue to get support and funds as you iterate from idea to your first ten customers; and

- brings clarity and alignment to all groups involved in the innovation journey.

Now that you understand the importance of getting Strategic Alignment, let's discuss how to get that alignment.

GET AGREEMENT ON A CUSTOMER BUSINESS OUTCOME

I recommend a three-step approach for getting to an agreement:

1. Stakeholder interviews
2. Market trend exploration (optional)
3. Alignment workshops

Stakeholder Interviews

The first step is to schedule one-on-one meetings with each of the critical stakeholders in your organization. Your goal is to learn their perspective on why the company needs to launch a new product and what problem this product will solve for their customers. As you meet with department heads (e.g., sales, marketing, operations, IT, finance, customer success,

Strategic Alignment

engineering), you'll learn that everybody has a different understanding of the problem and a different idea on how the company should approach a solution. I've done this exercise at multiple companies, and I'm always amazed at the difference of opinions. Your job is to hear all the different perspectives and summarize what you've heard.

When conducting stakeholder interviews, keep in mind that your stakeholders are busy and you might get only 15 to 30 minutes of their time. To make the most of your time with them, make sure to do your homework beforehand, including learning everything you can about the role of each stakeholder and how their department contributes to the overall company vision. You don't want to schedule time with a VP or C-level executive and start the conversation by asking them who they are and what they do at the company. It's OK to ask for clarifications if needed, but make sure you are well informed before going to the meeting. Believe me, you don't want to come across as wasting their time.

> **PRO TIP:** These initial interviews are crucial for building your credibility and trust with influential stakeholders. You will need their support later in your journey, so start building rapport by making them feel heard and included in the process.

Open the stakeholder interview by introducing yourself and reiterating the objective of the meeting. It is important to set up the context of why you are meeting with them and how you will use the information you gather. Let them know that you are in the Strategic Alignment stage of the B2B Innovator's Map and that you'll use this information as input for an alignment workshop you will conduct in the coming weeks that will include them and a few other key stakeholders.

Here are some useful questions you can use to gather insights during the stakeholder interview:

1. What is the biggest challenge our customers face today?

2. How is our company addressing that challenge today?

3. If we were to build a new product to address that challenge, what would that do for our company?

4. What would that new product mean for you and your organization?

5. Is there anything else you'd like to share?

As you interview your stakeholders, take the time to gather the market evidence they are using to justify the need for a particular product or problem to solve. In many cases, you'll find that their assumptions are informed by existing customers or by their knowledge of industry trends. If your stakeholders are basing their assumptions on market information, that's a great indicator that they are looking to solve customer problems, as opposed to internal business problems. If that is the case, then you can jump directly to step three and plan your alignment workshop. Otherwise, continue to the Market Trend Exploration step.

Market Trend Exploration (Optional)

If your stakeholders don't have market evidence to support their strategic direction, then it is useful to conduct a quick market trend exploration. Ideas for new products can come from anywhere, but the best ideas are the ones that exploit rapidly growing market trends in your industry. By researching relevant trends, you can identify some promising opportunities and use those as a starting point for the alignment workshops.

The market exploration doesn't need to be exhaustive. It just needs to give you enough information to drive the discussion during your alignment workshop. Here are some ideas for a quick market trend exploration:

- Talk to a handful of existing customers to understand their most pressing business challenges.

- Purchase or download free samples of analyst reports in your industry. These reports usually include the top challenges of a particular industry.

- Talk to an analyst directly to get their perspective of the challenges of a particular market. If you are not able to talk to one directly, you can always find free articles or podcasts by these same analysts. Remember that your goal is not to go very deep, but just to get enough information to start your journey.

Simply talking to a few customers and reading a few reports from industry analysts will give you enough information to get the conversations going. The opportunities you discover might leverage market, technology, or regulatory disruptions. But regardless of where the opportunity comes from, you should focus on understanding the customer outcomes that these trends enable and use that information in the alignment workshops to probe if that's a customer outcome your company would like to focus on.

Alignment Workshops

The last step is to facilitate workshops with all stakeholders to discuss what you learned during the one-on-one meetings and to highlight the difference of opinions. The workshops aim to align everybody on the company's priority and on the customer business outcome to pursue.

There are many ways to run these workshops. The format, duration, and facilitation approach will depend on your company's culture and personal style. The content of the workshops will

Strategic Alignment

revolve around affinity mapping exercises. **Affinity mapping is a facilitation technique that organizes similar ideas together to uncover underlying themes.** During the workshop, your goal is to collaborate with your stakeholders to rank the opportunities they believe the company should focus on and then discuss the emerging themes.

Here's the structure I use to run these alignment workshops:

1. Before the workshop, have a one-on-one conversation with each stakeholder to understand what customer business outcome they believe the company should focus on.

2. At the beginning of the workshop, walk everybody through the six stages of the B2B Innovator's Map. Point out that the goal of the day's workshop is to focus on stage one, Strategic Alignment. That way, you'll keep everybody focused on the task at hand, and you'll ensure that your stakeholders understand you are just at the beginning of this journey.

3. Using sticky notes, ask each stakeholder to write down the problem statement they believe the company should focus on. Ask every stakeholder to paste their sticky note(s) on a wall for everybody to see.

4. Group the sticky notes that address the same problem.

5. Facilitate a discussion to understand why multiple stakeholders suggest different problems to tackle. This is an excellent time to leverage the insights you learned during your one-on-one stakeholder interviews and your market trend research.

6. After hearing all the arguments, ask all stakeholders to vote on their top choice. Repeat this process until there is agreement on a single problem to go after.

As you work with your stakeholders to prioritize the customer outcome to pursue, make sure the discussion focuses on a customer outcome rather than an internal business goal. Here are a few examples of internal-facing goals that often show up during the alignment workshops:

- **Based on metrics:** "We need to grow our revenue by 35 percent, so we need a new product."

- **Based on trends:** "We need to innovate using AI."

- **Based on competitors:** "Our main competitor just moved into a new industry. We need a product to compete with them."

These problem areas are not actionable because they are "inward-facing." They focus on solving a problem for *your*

Strategic Alignment

company, such as more revenue or market share, instead of focusing on solving a *customer* problem. If you encounter such statements, guide the discussion towards converting any inward-facing objectives into customer-facing issues.

In contrast, here are some examples that focus on supporting a customer business outcome:

- "Our new product will help companies become more efficient at tracking their assets."

- "A new product will make it easier for companies to take payments over the internet."

- "Our goal is to enter a new market by creating a product that helps our customers save energy on their utility bills."

- "We want to help marketing teams get more ROI from their advertisement campaigns."

- "Our goal is to create a new line of products to help companies manage their human capital."

Although the problem statements above are still very high-level, they provide a great deal of direction for the innovation team. At this point, you don't have any information on which type of companies you'll be targeting, what kind of assets they are referring to, why it is hard to take payments over the internet, or what it means to get more ROI (return on investment) from an ad campaign. You'll answer all those questions at later stages of the innovation journey. During the Strategic Alignment stage, your only goal is to get agreement from the executive team on the high-level customer business outcome to explore.

Once you agree on the customer business outcome to explore, reserve a few minutes towards the end of the alignment workshop to explain that you've completed stage one of the innovation journey. You are now ready to move to stage two, Market Discovery. Take the time to explain the desired outcome of the Market Discovery stage and how your team will go about it. Also, make sure you emphasize that the customer business outcome you agreed to explore is only an assumption. During the Market Discovery stage, you might find there's no market or pain to solve in that area. Your stakeholders must understand that your initial assumption can be incorrect, and if that's the case, you'll get back together to agree on a new customer business outcome to explore.

Be aware that it might take several workshops to reach a consensus, but that's a good thing. The more engagement you get from all stakeholders, the more aligned they'll be and the better chance your product will have to succeed. The people in the room will become your allies and will help you when things get tough. Make sure you continue nurturing those relationships throughout the journey.

> **PRO TIP:** Since the goal of these workshops is to get alignment, I recommend having the innovation team (yourself and your team) lead these workshops. This is an opportunity for the innovation team to gain visibility, credibility, and trust as you drive this initiative forward. Many companies prefer to bring in a facilitator or hire an agency to do this alignment work. I don't recommend that. There will be time to leverage third-party vendors later in the process. Don't waste this opportunity!

ASSEMBLE YOUR INNOVATION TEAM

Now that you have an agreement on the customer problem to explore, it's time to secure a team to do that work. Many companies confuse the internal agreement of the problem to solve with a green light to start the development effort. Therefore, they assemble an entire product development team to begin building "the product." By now, you know that this approach leads to failure because you don't have any objective customer evidence on what the customer pain is and how you could solve it.

Instead, you need a small, dedicated team of innovators to focus on exploration. As you advance to later stages of the journey, your innovation team will continue to grow. But for now, you only need a handful of people with critical skills, including:

- Product management

- User research

- Interaction design

- Software development

- Business development

- Subject matter expertise on the target industry

Notice that I recommend "a handful of people with critical skills," not specifically people with those titles. What I mean is that this early in the process, your goal is to invest as little time and money as possible to find the answers you need. If your initial innovation team only has two people who, together, have the necessary skills, then you should start there. If you need three or four people, that's OK too. The goal is not to build a bloated team. As you gather customer evidence and start moving into the solution stages (stages four through six), then your team will grow, and you'll need seasoned professionals from all those disciplines. Until then, it's best to start small.

Strategic Alignment

Notice I also recommend a "dedicated" team. If your company agreed to explore a particular customer outcome, then part of that agreement is to provide the resources (people, time, funds) to conduct that exploration. The core responsibility of your innovation team is to explore those opportunities. It's their full-time job, not something they do once a week or between meetings when they have time. If your company is not willing to assign a few dedicated people to explore new opportunities, then you know they are not serious about innovation, and you might as well close the project right then and there.

CREATE AN ADVISORY BOARD

Building a new product requires the involvement and support of many departments across your organization. The more people you involve throughout the innovation journey, the better your chances of success will be. The opposite is also true. If you don't include anybody else in your journey, then your product will surely fail.

Therefore, now is the perfect time to create an Advisory Board in addition to assembling your innovation team. The goal of your Advisory Board is to secure support and constant involvement from your key stakeholders throughout the journey. I call it an Advisory Board, but feel free to give it a name that resonates with your company's culture. Other common names include the governance board or innovation council. Although these names sound very formal, the reality is that your Advisory Board is just a group of key stakeholders within your company who have an interest in supporting your innovation journey. If you work at a big company, your Advisory Board might include decision-makers from several business units. And if you work at a startup, your Advisory Board might just be your CEO and a couple of your peers. Your Advisory Board must include the key decision-maker in your company, meaning the person who has the final say on whether to continue, pivot, cancel, or move to the next stage of the innovation journey.

What the Advisory Board should expect from you:

- Keep them in the loop at a regular cadence to share your progress and solicit their feedback.

- Create a cadence to share any relevant market and customer insights.

- Call on them to make critical decisions (like go/no go decisions or support when moving from one stage to another).

What you should expect from your Advisory Board:

- Provide advice throughout the innovation journey.

- Approve your proposed next steps based on the insights you present.

Strategic Alignment

- Support your journey with resources (their time, budget, access to experts on their teams, political air cover, etc.).

The people on your Advisory Board will become your internal champions, so make sure you invite influential leaders and executives known for getting things done across your organization. I recommend having a diverse Advisory Board with representation from multiple departments (e.g., engineering, marketing, sales, legal, procurement).

> **PRO TIP:** If critical executives can't find the time to participate in the initiative, that is a big red flag. That signals that the initiative is low-priority for them, and without their support, your new product might not have a future even if you get all the way to stage six.

If you cannot get the support of key stakeholders, the best course of action is to escalate to your executive sponsor and try to figure out a solution. Do not move forward to the Market Discovery stage or you'll be spinning your wheels doing work that might not have a future in your company. Lack of internal support will derail your project sooner or later, so it's better to push the issue early on before you spend months going through the innovation journey.

AGREE ON PROGRESS METRICS

The last critical piece of the Strategic Alignment stage is to agree with your stakeholders on how you will measure and report progress. Most companies are not familiar with the innovation process, so they revert to using the metrics they know. These metrics include revenue targets and technology deliverables (i.e., new features of a product). These metrics are helpful when your product is more mature and your goal is to grow. But these metrics do not apply when you are this early in the innovation journey.

Early in the innovation journey, you need to focus on exploring potential opportunities, and therefore, you should be measured by your ability to gather customer evidence and reduce risk. As you advance through the various stages of the journey, your metrics will change to reflect the output of each stage.

Here are a few examples of useful metrics for every stage of the innovation journey.

The Market Discovery stage aims to select a target market to go after and get a deep understanding of the Champion in this market. Measurable metrics include:

- Number of markets you evaluate

- Number of potential markets you select

- Number of Champions you talk to

Strategic Alignment

The goal of the **User Discovery** stage is to understand the User Ecosystem in your target market. Measurable metrics include:

- Number of interviews you conduct to identify the key players in your User Ecosystem

- Whether these interviews are converging or diverging into a problem you could solve

The goal of the **Solution Planning** stage is to create your Solution Diagram and experimentation roadmap. Measurable metrics include:

- Ability to get buy-in on your Solution Diagram from the Advisory Board

- Number of assumptions in your experimentation roadmap and your plan to test them

The goal of the **Prototyping** stage is to test your hypothesis and start building your product based on customer evidence. Measurable metrics include:

- Speed of iterating and testing your prototypes

- How these prototypes are helping you converge or diverge on the customer problem

The goal of the **Early Adopter** stage is to deliver value to your first ten customers. You can also incorporate some early business development metrics since you'll need a pipeline with leads that you can convert into your first ten customers. Measurable metrics include:

- How effective you are in delivering value to your first ten customers

- Number of customers in your business development pipeline and their likelihood to convert to one of your first ten paid customers

The metrics and progress milestones I listed above should give you an idea of what you could propose to your leadership team. Feel free to play around with these metrics and make sure you propose something that feels doable for your team. Remember that innovation is filled with uncertainty, so chances are you will miss your metrics the first few times until you start gaining confidence with the process. By agreeing on metrics early on, you'll be setting your team up for success, and you'll be setting the right cadence with your leadership team on what to expect at each stage of the innovation journey.

REAL-WORLD STORY

Sebastian was Director of Engineering at an enterprise medical software company. The company's executives had heard about the potential of machine learning (ML) in the medical space, so they decided to explore potential opportunities. With great fanfare, they announced a brand-new innovation lab to

Strategic Alignment

create the next generation of products that would disrupt the company from the inside. The executive team seemed very serious about this initiative. Not only did they assign Sebastian to lead this lab, but they rented a big and beautiful space in the heart of Silicon Valley so they could attract talent (and media attention). The lab also came with a couple dozen engineers and a few million dollars to "innovate."

But for all the resources the company was investing in the new lab, there was one critical item missing: the Strategic Alignment on what the innovation lab should produce. The only direction Sebastian received was to "go innovate." Sebastian had a data science background, so he was well aware of the potential of ML, but without clear direction, he didn't know what areas or use-cases to focus on first. At the same time, he had the pressure of keeping his new engineering team "busy" building the next big thing, even if they didn't know what that should be.

Sebastian had several conversations with his leadership team, but he wasn't able to get any specific direction. Each of the stakeholders was only interested in getting "quick wins" for their business unit. They wanted the innovation lab to produce something fast to help them meet their current revenue goals. In addition, Sebastian learned that each stakeholder was interested in exploring different industries and use cases, which made it harder to know where to begin.

Sebastian then tried the opposite approach. Instead of trying to get direction from his leadership team, he thought of doing some research and coming up with a few exciting opportunities to propose to his executive team. After a few weeks of exploration, Sebastian presented a list of potential opportunities he saw in the market to create new products leveraging ML. To his surprise, his presentation fell flat. The leadership team had objections to each of the areas Sebastian proposed. The objections ranged from "We don't want to go into that market" to "We don't think there's potential there." But these objections were based on "gut feelings," as opposed to objective customer evidence. At the end of the meeting, the leadership team put it back to Sebastian to come up with something "innovative" they could get behind.

For the next few months, Sebastian kept playing more rounds of innovation theater. His company was involved in the illusion of innovation, but they had nothing to show for it. A year into the initiative, the leadership team decided to cancel the lab and move their funding back to their core business to generate more revenue they could include in their quarterly report. Just like that, Sebastian went back to his old role of Director of Engineering, and the innovation lab was soon forgotten. The only time it was mentioned was to say that the company had tried innovation, but it didn't work for them.

This story is widespread for both established companies trying to "innovate" and for startups that don't have clarity on the customer problem they need to solve. Large companies can take the hit of time and money lost in the name of "innovation," but

Strategic Alignment

this innovation theater hits startups harder because they tend to run out of funds before producing anything meaningful.

From this real-world story, it is easy to see why Strategic Alignment needs to be the first step in any innovation journey. Without an explicit agreement on the problem to solve and strong support from the leadership team on investing in this journey, the whole initiative is destined to fail. Unfortunately, most companies start their journey at the Prototyping or Early Adopter stages of the innovation journey, meaning they begin building a product out of a single idea, and in most cases, that idea fails.

If you find yourself in Sebastian's shoes, make sure you work with your leadership team to explain the various stages of the journey between idea and your first ten customers. Get their buy-in into what it will take to launch a new product. If you don't get this Strategic Alignment, save everybody some heartburn and kill the initiative right there. Otherwise, you'll risk becoming part of an executive pet project, but you'll have nothing to show for your efforts.

If you have alignment on what business outcome to explore, have support from your key stakeholders, and agree on the progress metrics to use, congratulations! You have completed stage one of the innovation journey. Now it's time to start exploring who has the most significant pain in the area you selected. In other words, it's time to move to stage two of the innovation journey, Market Discovery.

Learn More

Below are some of my favorite books to help you get alignment across your company:

- *High-Impact Tools for Teams: 5 Tools to Align Team Members, Build Trust, and Get Results Fast* by Stefano Mastrogiacomo and Alexander Osterwalder

- *Zone to Win: Organizing to Compete in an Age of Disruption* by Geoffrey Moore

- *Pirates In The Navy: How Innovators Lead Transformation* by Tendayi Viki

- *How to Win Friends and Influence People* by Dale Carnegie

Those books will give you additional tools and enable you to fine-tune your innovation language so that you can focus on bringing your company together.

Note: Get an extended list of books, the companion workbook, and additional resources by downloading your B2B Innovator's Kit at https://danielelizalde.com/b2b-innovators-kit.

Chapter 3

Market Discovery

I ONCE ADVISED A COMPANY WORKING ON ENERGY EFFICIENCY solutions. They had amazing technology, but the Product team was struggling to prioritize the features they should build next. I noticed that their roadmap was all over the place, so I asked their head of products, "Who is your target market?" He said, "Anybody who wants to improve their energy efficiency." That was a big red flag for me. "What do you mean by 'anybody'?" I asked. "Well," he said, "buildings, homes, you name it." No wonder they had trouble prioritizing features!

By focusing on "anybody" they were serving "nobody." The problem was that this company had not selected a target market, and therefore, they had no strategy. As I continued to probe deeper, he mentioned that their technology works for buildings of all sizes, so they didn't want to leave money on the table by focusing on a particular type of building or even homes.

Unfortunately, the fear of missing out always backfires. Although the technology might work for any type of building, the needs of the Champion for each type of building are very different. For example, the needs (and therefore the type of solution) for school buildings will be different from hotels, and different from supermarkets or airports. They are all "buildings," but the use-cases are radically different.

By not focusing on a particular target market, they missed out on understanding the needs of a specific target audience, and therefore, they struggled in building a product they could validate with ten customers of one particular market.

When you select a target market, prioritizing your roadmap, as well as aligning the rest of the organization (including sales and marketing) behind your product, becomes much easier. In fact, any time you struggle with any part of the product development cycle, look back at whether you have a clear understanding of your target market. Believe me, most downstream issues in product development can be traced back to a lack of focus on who you are serving and what problem you are solving for them.

In the Strategic Alignment stage, you agreed with your company on the customer business outcome you plan to explore. The purpose of the Market Discovery stage is to gather market evidence on which type of customer is experiencing the biggest pain related to that business outcome, what

Market Discovery

market they are in, and how big that market is. In short, the goal of the Market Discovery stage is to select a target market and evaluate its potential to support your new business.

On the innovation journey, you are here:

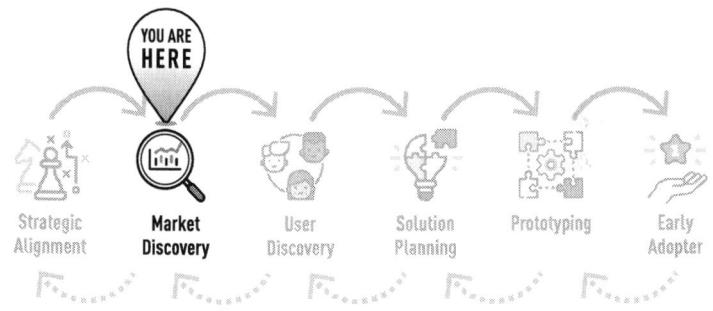

By the end of the Market Discovery stage, you'll have a clear understanding of the best market to go after, and you will have a deep understanding of the needs of the Champions in that market. To get there, I've broken down this stage into four steps:

1. Select your target market

2. Research your target market's size

3. Understand your Champion's needs

4. Get buy-in on your target market

Let's look at each step in more detail.

SELECT YOUR TARGET MARKET

A target market is a group of companies with similar characteristics, that are experiencing a similar pain, and can leverage your product to make progress towards a business outcome. By focusing on companies from the same target market, you'll quickly learn whether the problem you are exploring is prevalent in that market or not.

For companies to be in the same target market, they need to share these components:

- Industry

- Company size

- Geography

- Champion

- Use case

When getting started with the Market Discovery stage, you might need to cast a wider net and explore several markets until you discover the market with the most potential. Just remember to keep narrowing your focus from several markets into a single market to explore.

Market Discovery

Many companies avoid narrowing down to a single target market because they fear missing out on some opportunities. Instead of focusing on a specific target market, they aim for whatever customer they can get. Therefore, their first ten customers belong to different industries, have various use cases, and include any size company, from startups to large enterprises. This approach is wasteful because companies in different markets have different challenges, so you won't know if the pain you are exploring is pervasive in that market or not. **The sooner you can agree with your company on a single target market to explore, the more efficiently you will utilize your resources in the upcoming stages of the innovation journey.**

> **PRO TIP:** Your leadership team might be hesitant to focus on one particular market because of the fear of missing out. Remind them that once your product gains traction in your initial target market, there will be opportunities to grow horizontally to other markets. But that comes much later than your first ten customers. For now, it is more important to stay focused and apply all your energy to exploring your most promising target market first.

When exploring potential markets, your choice of industry anchors your selection process because industry is the component with the most variability. From there, each subsequent component, such as company size and geography, continues to narrow down your target market.

Let's use an example to illustrate the importance of selecting companies within the same target market. Assume that during the Strategic Alignment stage, your company agrees to explore the problem of "helping companies become more efficient at tracking assets." Increasing your customer's efficiency is an excellent business outcome to explore, but it is not actionable.

To be actionable, you need to answer questions like:

- What types of "companies" are you talking about?

- Who, within that company, has the problem?

- What kind of "assets" are you going to track?

Your product will be very different if you track vaccine delivery, versus tracking packages in a warehouse, versus tracking cellular radios across a city, versus tracking people (human assets) coming in and out of buildings. These are all "tracking" applications, but they are all in different target markets because they span multiple industries and use cases—not to mention that the characteristics of the Champion in the healthcare industry (tracking vaccine delivery) will be very different from one in the telecommunications industry (tracking cellular radios).

Market Discovery

Without clarity on the target market, you can't define any next steps for your teams. How do you research the pains of "users within companies"? What kind of technology do you need to track "assets"?

You can bring clarity to your teams by defining the components of the target market to go after. For the asset tracking example, you can define your target market as:

- **Industry:** retail

- **Company size:** Fortune 500 companies (10,000+ employees)

- **Geography:** United States

- **Champion:** warehouse manager (the role of the person responsible for achieving the customer's business outcome)

- **Use case:** track packages inside warehouses

With this information, you can evolve the statement you created during the Strategic Alignment stage from "helping companies become more efficient at tracking assets" to something more specific and actionable, like "helping warehouse managers working at Fortune 500 retailers in the United States to track packages inside warehouses."

Each component of the target market plays a critical role in narrowing down the scope of your new product. In the example below, notice how changing any of these components puts you in a different target market and would significantly impact the solution you need to build to meet the needs of that market.

- **Changing industry:** The challenges of tracking packages in the retail industry will differ from tracking packages in the healthcare or aviation industry, resulting in very different products.

- **Changing company size:** The requirements of large organizations are very different from startups or small- to medium-sized businesses—not to mention that larger companies have significantly more complicated internal processes and have more people involved in their User Ecosystem.

- **Changing geography:** Changes in geography have a significant impact on the product strategy, especially when it comes to deployment, regulation, compliance, and localization, just to name a few.

- **Changing Champion:** The goal of your enterprise software product is to support the needs of a Champion. Changing the

Champion means building a completely different product for a different set of requirements. In the example above, a warehouse manager's challenges are very different from a COO's or security guard's challenges, even if they all work at the same company. As you explore a target market, you may discover that the person responsible for the business outcome is not the same one you assumed. In this case, you are not changing target markets. You are just refining your understanding of the same market by fine-tuning the characteristics of your Champion.

- **Changing use case:** Tracking inventory vs. tracking delivery trucks vs. tracking people inside a warehouse each requires very different solutions. The context of the use case is also essential. In this case, tracking packages inside the warehouse is also very different from tracking packages in transit.

A common mistake is to be very generic with the definition of the target market components. For example, selecting the company size as "large" or "enterprise" is not helpful. These generalizations won't help you make decisions because they are too ambiguous. How large is "large"? How big or small is an "enterprise?" When defining the company size, I suggest using something you can measure, such as annual revenue or the number of employees. **The more specific you are**

with each of the components of your target market, the easier the rest of the process will be.

Here's an example of a potential starting point for your exploration.

	Potential Target Market One	Potential Target Market Two	Potential Target Market Three
Industry	Manufacturing	Manufacturing	Manufacturing
Company size	$10M	$100M	$100M
Geography	USA	USA	USA
Champion	Plant Manager	Plant Manager	Plant Manager
Use case	Control large machinery	Control large machinery	Control pumps

In this example, I'm highlighting the components that change across each of my potential target markets. Ideally, you want to propose target markets that are similar (i.e., only one component is different between them) so that you can make fast progress on evaluating each one. Changing two or more components between these target markets will force you to go much deeper to assess their potential.

If you don't have a sense of which markets might be the best for you to explore, it's OK to propose markets that are completely different from each other. For example, you can explore the need of asset tracking in the supply chain industry, in the medical industry, and the mining industry. At this stage, you are working on exploration, so if your company needs to go wide before you can go narrow, that's OK. Just remember that your goal is to narrow down your focus so your first ten customers can all be part of the same target market. Carrying forward multiple target markets to further stages of the innovation journey will exponentially increase the variables you need to test, and therefore, it'll make it harder (not easier) to identify the best opportunities for your new product.

Now that you have selected one (or a few) potential markets to explore, it's time to see if this market is big enough to support your new business.

RESEARCH YOUR TARGET MARKET SIZE

Before jumping in to explore a particular target market, it's critical to estimate how big that market is. There is no clear threshold on what constitutes a "big" or a "small" market. What is big for some companies might be small for others. The key is to understand if that market is large enough to support your company's new business and attractive enough to your investors or executive team.

A common mistake is to confuse the size of a market category with the size of your target market. Market category refers to a type of solution, such as CRM, human capital management (HCM), or cloud computing. The revenue potential in these categories is enormous because they include all industries, company sizes, geographies, and use cases for that type of solution. Your investors and executive teams will want to know the potential of the market category. Still, you need to bring them back to reality and focus on the size of the specific target market you are proposing.

TAM and SAM

The size of your target market, also known as total addressable market (TAM), represents the total potential revenue from all the companies in that specific market, assuming you get 100 percent of that market. Continuing with our example, "asset tracking" is a market category since it includes tracking any type of asset in any industry. And that number is enormous. In this case, we want to estimate the TAM for Fortune 500 retailers in the United States looking to track packages inside a warehouse. This number will not be as large as the size for the total market category, but it should be large enough to justify your company's investment.

To calculate the TAM, you can use this formula:

TAM = number of companies that meet your target market criteria × revenue you could get from each company

Be aware that the amount of revenue you could get from each company is a big assumption since you are early in the Market Discovery stage. You'll learn more about how to price your offering and your customer's willingness to pay during the

Market Discovery

Prototyping stage. If your stakeholders require more detailed information, you can go deeper from the TAM and calculate the serviceable addressable market (SAM), which is the portion of the total market you believe your product can capture.

> **PRO TIP:** You don't need to be very precise with the TAM or SAM numbers at this stage because there are too many unknowns for your calculations to be believable. What you are after is the sense of whether your target market is big enough to justify your company's investment, so don't go overboard.

When communicating the size of your proposed target market to your investors or executive team, make sure you combine the big-picture opportunity with the reality of where you are in the process. This means:

1. Presenting data that justifies the target market having potential (TAM and SAM).

2. Reiterating that once your product gets traction in this initial target market, your company will be able to expand to other markets. But at this point, you will need to start small by laser-focusing on a specific market.

3. Reminding them that your critical milestone is to get ten customers in one target market. This will help your company reduce risks and have a better chance to succeed in this and future markets.

> **PRO TIP:** If your resulting TAM is too small, you can broaden your scope by modifying any component of your target market (e.g., industry, company size, geography, use case) to look for a more attractive market size.

Where to Get Information About Your Target Market

If your company is already operating in the same target market you are proposing, your product marketing team might already have some market size information. If you are looking at a different industry, company size, or geography, you might need to get that information from another source. The fastest way to get there is by talking to industry analysts. Chances are they've already done this research and can save you a lot of time.

Industry analysts can help you answer questions like:

- How big is a particular market (i.e., how many potential customers you could have)?

Market Discovery

- Which business outcomes are top of mind for this market?

- What are some specific titles for the Champions in this market?

- Which use cases are gaining traction in which industries and geographies?

- Which companies are already in that market (i.e., your competition)?

- What is the average spend from companies in this market to achieve their desired business outcome?

Working with analyst firms can be very expensive. Since you are very early in your innovation journey, I don't recommend hiring analyst firms to conduct a custom research project. At this point, you can get all the information you need by buying one of their existing reports and paying to get a few analysts on the phone for short interviews. Another way to move fast is to talk to a subject matter expert on that market from within your company. Hopefully, your innovation team or Advisory Board would include one of these subject matter experts (SMEs), so this is a great time to engage them.

Keep in mind that your goal is to get this information as quickly as possible to move forward to the next step of the innovation journey. Your goal is *not* to become an expert on the market or generate another 1,000-slide deck that nobody will read.

Once you have enough information to confirm (or deny) that the size of your proposed target market is attractive, meet with your Advisory Board to share your progress and get their buy-in on the target market you plan to explore. If there are concerns about that target market, it is better to surface them now.

Now that you've selected a target market to explore and you have some evidence that the market is big enough to support your new business, the next step is to deep-dive into this market to get a clear understanding of your Champion's needs.

UNDERSTAND YOUR CHAMPION'S NEEDS

Most companies believe that selecting a target market gives you enough information to build and launch a product. And that's precisely why most new products fail. At this point, you have general information about a market, but you still don't have a deep understanding of the pain your Champion in that market is experiencing.

For example, the problem statement for the asset tracking example I used before was: "Helping warehouse managers working at Fortune 500 retailers in the United States to track packages inside a warehouse." This statement has all the components of a target market definition, but it is still not actionable. It is still missing the "why."

Why do those managers need to track packages inside the warehouse? And *why* would they be willing to invest in a new

Market Discovery

tracking solution? In other words, what is the core pain they are experiencing?

You might start with the assumption that warehouse managers need to track packages in their warehouses to fulfill orders (i.e., inventory-related problems), so their challenges revolve around operational efficiency. But it is possible that after talking to a few of them, you discover they are losing a lot of money to stolen packages. Their core pain is around theft management and not inventory management, as you had imagined.

My point is that **you cannot know the core pain of your Champions until you talk to them**. If you don't speak directly to your prospects, you are only guessing their pains, and you will let your personal and company bias drive the innovation process.

There is no magic formula for figuring out your Champion's pain. The only way to discover their pain is to talk to them. But how do you do it?

To understand the pains of your Champions, you need a structured approach to gather the information you need. This structured approach includes knowing:

1. Which questions to ask

2. How to engage your Champions

3. Where to find Champions to engage with

Let's dive into each of these areas.

Which Questions to Ask

Below are four powerful questions that will help you get to the core of your Champion's needs. Your goal is to ask these questions from as many Champions in your target market as you can:

1. What is your biggest pain around _____?
2. Where, when, and how often is the problem occurring?
3. What is the impact of that pain?
4. What are you doing today to mitigate that pain?

Let me break down each of these questions to show you why they are important and the outcome you want from each one of them.

1. What Is Your Biggest Pain Around _____?

This question is a conversation starter that cuts right into your Champion's pain. Using the warehouse example, you could phrase the question as, "What is your biggest pain around tracking packages inside your warehouses?"

Market Discovery

After asking this question, it's OK to ask follow-up questions to clarify or get more specifics, but overall, let the customer do the talking. You are there to learn. I've seen conversations where the interviewer picks up on a customer's pain and immediately goes into "sales mode," explaining how their (future) solution will solve that problem. By going into "sales mode," you are turning the focus back to yourself and your potential product as opposed to focusing on your customer's pains. The more you focus on listening, the more insights you will find, and the better product you'll be able to build.

Also, don't try to steer the conversation back to what you "think" you want to learn. For example, I remember when my team and I conducted a series of Champion interviews with hotel operations managers. The interview went something like this:

My team: What is your biggest pain around saving energy?

Champion: Saving energy is important, but we have that covered. What I struggle with is having leaky toilets. Do you have anything to help me with that?

This exchange was eye-opening because it revealed that the customer's top concern was not remotely aligned with the problem we were trying to solve. That is precious information, and if you have too many interviews like that, you know that the issue you are looking to solve is not painful enough for your customer. That'd be your cue to select a different target market or go back to the Strategic Alignment stage to agree on another customer business outcome to explore.

> **PRO TIP:** A great follow-up question is, "Who else in your organization is experiencing the pain?" Their answer will give you a more holistic view of your customer's world. Plus, this information will be invaluable during the User Discovery stage as you map out your User Ecosystem.

2. Where, When, and How Often Is the Problem Occurring?

It's essential to understand the context of the problem to formulate the best possible solution. As you talk to various Champions, make sure to ask where the problem occurs, when it happens (at night, at day, after a change in shift, etc.), and how often it occurs.

Your goal is to build a clear, step-by-step scenario of how the issue shows up in your customer's world. The best way to get this scenario is by asking your Champion to walk you through the last time the pain happened. That way, you are asking for a concrete example and you'll get a rich story that describes the situation. Make sure you probe to understand what happened before, during, and after the issue occurred.

Market Discovery

The details of this story will give you a lot of valuable information about your Champions' needs, and about how they felt throughout the whole incident. The emotional component is very important because people buy based on emotion, not logic. The more you can get to that emotion, the better your customer understanding will be.

3. What Is the Impact of the Problem?

This question helps you understand the consequence and magnitude that this pain has in your Champion's life.

You can group the majority of B2B desired outcomes into three categories:

1. Increasing revenue

2. Reducing cost

3. Reducing risk

With this question, your first objective is to learn how this pain affects your Champion (revenue, cost, risk) and what metrics they use to measure that pain. Your second objective is to understand the magnitude of the impact. Is this simply an annoyance they can live with? Or is it something that disrupts their operations and affects their bottom line? Understanding the impact helps you understand the value your customers might place in solving this issue, which will give you insight into their willingness to pay for a solution.

To understand the impact of the pain, ask follow-up questions until you get to the root of the pain. Here's an example exchange with a hotel manager (Champion) about the impact of complying with new building efficiency regulations.

You: What is the impact of the new building efficiency regulations?

Hotel manager: It will have a significant impact because we will need to redesign our sustainability strategy to stay below the new government targets for CO2 emissions.

You: How does that impact your business?

Hotel manager: If we cannot meet the new CO2 emission standard, we'll have to pay a hefty penalty.

You: And what is the impact of that?

Hotel manager: To avoid the penalty, we need to go beyond the low-hanging fruit of changing light bulbs and such. We need to invest in more efficient furnaces and chillers. Plus, we need to find additional efficiencies anywhere we can.

You: What is the impact of having to update your equipment?

Hotel manager: Well, it's not about the cost of changing the equipment since we planned to do that anyway. We don't

Market Discovery

have a reliable way to measure the CO2 contribution of the various parts of the building, plus we don't have any tools to track our progress. So, the impact is not only paying for the improvements we need; it's also purchasing the tools to evaluate and track our progress, plus the expense of training our staff to conduct the audits to meet the regulation.

As you can see, you were able to get to the real impact of the problem with these questions. Without this level of inquiry, you could have assumed that the impact was just around the finances of buying more efficient equipment. But by asking follow-up questions, you learned that the impact is also about implementing a new process and getting the tools and training necessary to comply with the regulation.

As you dig deeper with each follow-up question, aim to quantify your Champion's pain to understand if it is a $10 problem or a $10M problem. Without this information, your team can over-engineer the product and end up with a more expensive solution than the cost of living with the pain.

Keep in mind that the problem's size must be proportional to the companies or departments you are targeting. If you target multi-billion-dollar corporations, a $10M problem might be just a nuisance, and they might not be willing to invest in a new solution.

> **PRO TIP:** If your Champion is not measuring or tracking the impact or potential savings of this pain, that is an indication that the pain is not big enough.

4. What Are You Doing Today to Mitigate This Pain?

Understanding how your Champion is solving a problem today is a significant indicator that the problem is real. Learning about their current approach gives you a sense of the magnitude of the problem, their willingness to pay, and the competition you are against.

Sometimes Champions start talking about a particular problem, but when you ask what they are doing about it, they say, "Oh, nothing really." That's a clear indicator that the problem is not big enough and that if you were to come up with a solution for that problem, your customer might not buy it. Think about it this way, if your Champion is not doing anything to solve that pain, how big of a pain is it?

On the other hand, if they share with you a list of solutions they've tried or tell you they've hired people to tackle the issue, then you know the pain is real. This opens the door for a rich conversation about what works, what doesn't, and what opportunities you might have to fill in the gaps.

Now that you know the four critical questions to ask, let's talk about the best ways to engage with your Champions to get the answers you need.

How to Engage Your Champions

Although there are many ways to engage with your customers, the best techniques are the ones where you can interact directly with your Champions, which include:

- On-site visits
- Interviews
- Surveys

Let me describe each of them along with their pros, cons, and when to use them.

On-Site Visits

The best way to understand your Champion's pain is to watch them struggle with that pain in their environment. That's why conducting on-site visits is my favorite method for understanding what your customer needs.

On-site visits consist of scheduling time to visit your prospect in person at their facility or wherever they are experiencing the pain. By visiting them in their environment, you can pick up on many subtle cues on how they go about their day, the context they work in, what type of tools they use, what their office looks like, who they work with, etc. You can even discover additional challenges they have that might open the door to new products.

On-site visits will always give you the most amount of detail about your customer's world. But they are not always possible due to location, budget, or customer availability. Depending on your industry, some customers might not be authorized to have visitors, or the visit might not be practical (think about hospitals, military contractors, or airplane pilots). If you find yourself in this situation, you can always rely on interviews and surveys.

Interviews

Interviews are a powerful tool for diving deeper or following up after an on-site visit. Your team can conduct these interviews in person (at your facility, trade show, coffee shop, etc.) or remotely via phone or video conference.

One benefit of interviews is that you can work with your team to create an interview map outlining the key topics of your conversation and reuse the same interview map with many participants worldwide. These interviews, especially the remote ones, can be a great way to cover a lot of ground

Market Discovery

very quickly since your team can interview dozens of participants in a single week. Having multiple interviews in a short amount of time allows your team to quickly determine whether you are converging into a common problem or if you are diverging and you need to regroup and rethink your approach.

Make sure a cross-functional team participates in these interviews. You'll get the most value if people listening to the interview have different backgrounds and vantage points, such as people from product, design, engineering, marketing, or sales. Sometimes it is not possible or practical to have multiple people participate in the interview. Therefore, ask permission to record the interview so others can listen to it later.

Surveys

Interviews give you a lot of qualitative information because they are based on open-ended questions. When conducting interviews, your team should start seeing convergence or divergence within eight to twelve participants, if not sooner.

Once you have that convergence, I recommend using surveys to test whether a larger group of people also has the same pain you've identified. **Surveys allow you to gather quantitative data to analyze convergence or divergence at a larger scale.**

You can also use surveys to prepare for on-site visits and interviews. You can use a survey to get a broad understanding of your target market and then use that information to refine the topics you'll discuss during interviews and on-site visits.

As a word of caution, make sure you use surveys to complement interviews and on-site visits and not as a replacement. Surveys provide valuable information, but they lack context, emotion, and the opportunity to dive into your customers' deeper "why." Also, make sure to avoid leading questions or provide survey answers that might bias the user towards your existing assumptions.

Where to Find Champions to Engage With

One of the biggest challenges of conducting Market Discovery for enterprise software is getting access to the people who can answer your questions. In the B2C world, it is a lot easier to find people to talk to because the applications are less specialized. You can park your team at a coffee shop and ask people passing by to answer a few questions, and you'd probably get good insights. But that doesn't work in the B2B world. In B2B, the specific roles you need to talk to are harder to reach, they are swamped, and any minute they spend with you is a minute they are not tending to their business.

So where do you start?

Market Discovery

Below is a list of recommendations on where to find people to talk to. Ensure everybody you speak to is part of your target market, including Champion, industry, company size, geography, and use case.

Start with Your Network

It's a lot easier to access people you know, so tapping into your network is a great place to start. When launching a new research project, organize a "network brainstorming" meeting with your team. The meeting's goal is to leverage your team's network to compile a list of people in your target market you could reach out to.

Find Proxies

There will be times when you won't find people in your exact target audience. This is expected, especially when you need to connect with very specialized roles or people very high up in the organization.

In this situation, you can look for proxies. Proxies are people related to your Champions. They can be your Champion's peers, their vendors, part of their staff (i.e., direct reports), people who used to perform that role but have moved on, etc.

Proxies can give you great insights, can point you in the right direction, and can connect you with other people to talk to.

Leverage Social Media

Social media might sound like a strange place to find B2B contacts, but believe me, it can be very productive. Once you identify which social media platform is the most relevant for your target audience, spend some time looking at popular articles and conversation threads to understand the main topics they are discussing. The article author might be an excellent person to interview to get deeper insights into their world. Also, pay attention to the comments within relevant posts to learn who is interested in these topics, as well as their feedback or objections. These are all people you could interact with and recruit for an interview.

Join Industry Groups

Every industry has interest groups where like-minded professionals get together to "talk shop," get advice, or network with other professionals. Some of those groups might be free. Others might be by invitation only, and others might be part of a paid membership to an organization or event. As part of the initial research on your target market, try to identify and join the most prominent industry groups. The more active you are in those groups, the easier it will be to recruit people who can help you answer your research questions.

> **PRO TIP:** The best way to uncover the top industry groups for your target market is to ask people in that target market. This is a great question to include in a survey or something you can bring up during an interview.

Contact Existing Customers and Prospects

Your company might already have a list of people who meet your research criteria. They might be existing customers or maybe leads collected from your website or other marketing events. These people could be great candidates to reach out to and have a conversation with. Work with your marketing team to send a survey to that prospect list. The survey can include an open-ended question about your research topic, as well as a question like, "Can we contact you to further discuss any of your answers?" If they say yes, congratulations! You just secured a new interview candidate.

Connect through Conferences

Conferences are great opportunities to connect with people in your target market. Before attending an event (in person or virtual), spend the time to craft a strategy on how to approach the event. Learn who is attending and who you could talk to.

Start by looking at the list of speakers. In most industry events, the speakers are usually practitioners, and they can be good candidates (or proxies) to interview. Just be respectful and mindful of their time.

> **PRO TIP:** You don't need to focus only on upcoming conferences. Your team can spend an afternoon mining event websites to compile a list of past speakers. Conference websites are a treasure trove of research opportunities.

When looking at conference websites, also pay attention to who the sponsors are. If the event is well aligned with your target market, then the list of sponsors can be another opportunity for your team to discuss if they know anybody at those companies.

Also, consider becoming a sponsor for a conference as a way to get access to the attendee list and network with other sponsors and vendors. Other invitation-only conferences might offer to share the attendees' list as a hook to get you to attend.

Engage with Agencies and Consultants

Some agencies specialize in connecting organizations with prominent experts in a particular field. These agencies can help you look for a specific profile that can be hard to get. But keep in mind that sometimes these companies will try to connect you with consultants, analysts, or industry experts. Although their input is valuable, they are a proxy to your Champion. They don't have the pain themselves, so you should use their feedback as a direction only.

Interview People from Your Own Company

I want to caution you against interviewing people from your own company who have similar roles or characteristics as your Champion. For example, if you are building a product for sales teams, you might be inclined to interview your own sales team. If your product is for developers, you might want to talk to your own development team. If you are researching manufacturing solutions and your company has a manufacturing team, your first inclination might be to speak to them.

On principle, this sounds like an excellent way to get started. But the reality is that you'll get very biased opinions on their problems, and often, these interviews will be heavily skewed towards solutions—your company's solution in particular.

As long as you know these biases, these interviews can serve as a warm-up exercise for interacting with the outside world. Also, these interviews can be a great way to get introductions to external people. They say "birds of a feather fly together," so it's very likely that people in your company can give you great info on what conferences they attend, an idea of where to find more people doing the same role, or connections to their friends at other companies.

Work with Sales to Get Access to Existing Customers or Prospects

Let's talk about the elephant in the room. In most companies selling enterprise software, the sales organization controls any access to customers and prospects. That means that anybody who wants to talk to a customer needs to get approval from sales. I've seen this to be true both at small startups with just a couple of sales people and at large organizations with large sales teams.

If you have asked sales for access to a few customers or prospects, you've probably heard things like:

- "Nobody talks to the customer except for sales."

- "Just tell me what you want to know, and I'll ask them."

- "Why talk to customers if you are not going to sell them anything?"

- "We've tried that before, and it was a disaster. We are not doing that again."

- "I'm not going to jeopardize a deal by having this interview."

- "We are supposed to be the experts. We can't go to a customer and ask them about their pain. We can't risk appearing like we don't know what we are doing."

It's easy to understand their perspective. The sales team is responsible for the relationship with the customer, and they've been burned before by product teams who didn't have the skills to conduct productive customer interviews. I've been there, and I'm sure you have too.

Convincing sales (or any other department) to give your team access to customers takes time and effort. Your focus should be on two areas: **trust** and **education**.

Before asking the sales team for their help, you need to earn their trust. They need to trust you will take care of their customer and that this interview will create more business for the company, not less. This trust is not earned overnight. It takes time and is usually based on the personal relationships you and your team have with your sales team.

The second part is education. Sometimes we get "*no*" for an answer because the salesperson might not be familiar with how the market discovery process works, the questions you want to ask, how the process of asking the questions works, and what you will do with that information.

Your goal is to make the sales team familiar (and comfortable) with:

- How your team will interact with their customer

- What types of questions you'll ask, and how you'll stay away from any pending deal

- How those insights eventually become a product they can sell (and earn commission)

- How these interactions strengthen the customer relationship

Once your sales team is familiar with the market discovery process, then it's a good idea to discuss rules of engagement for who, how, and when your team will talk to customers. Agreeing on an approach will help you strengthen the trust and continue to open the doors with your sales team.

As part of the education process, I recommend including sales leaders in your Advisory Board. Keep them in the loop and share the insights you are discovering throughout the process. Also, include people from the sales team in some of your interviews to experience the process and realize that the insights you are gaining will make for a better product they eventually can sell. In time, you'll build strong relationships, and as you know, there is no stronger ally than a sales leader in an enterprise company.

How Many People Should You Talk To?

I recommend aiming for eight to ten conversations with Champions in your target market. You are looking for similar answers to the question, "What is your biggest pain around ____?" If, after ten conversations, you get ten different answers, you know there is no convergence on the customer business outcome you selected. You should either refine your target market or go back to the Strategic Alignment stage to choose a different customer business outcome to explore.

If you get two to three convergent responses out of your ten interviews, then you might not have enough data to decide one way or another. In this case, you should conduct eight to ten additional interviews just to make sure you are filtering the signal from the noise. On the other hand, if most of the people you talk to complain about the same pain, you know you are onto something.

Now that you have all this information about your target market and potential Champion, you are ready to move to the last step of the Market Discovery stage. Assuming that your target market has promise, the last step of the Market Discovery stage is to get your company's final buy-in to continue exploring this opportunity.

> **NOTE:** This would be a good time to revisit the companion B2B Innovator's Workbook and make sure you haven't missed any important steps.

GET BUY-IN ON YOUR TARGET MARKET

Based on all the work you've done, you should have enough data to make the case to either move forward with or abandon this opportunity. But before you discuss your findings with your Advisory Board, it is important to spend time organizing your data and crafting your story. Data is never enough to get people to act. Data is just the supporting information that gives credibility to your story.

Craft a Story

Your goal is to create a short, compelling story around the customer pain you have identified. Think of it as your elevator pitch to justify why your company should continue exploring this opportunity.

Your story should incorporate all the elements you've collected so far, including:

- The customer business outcome your company has agreed to explore (from the Strategic Alignment stage)

Market Discovery

- The details of your target market (Champion, use case, industry, company size, and geography)

- Insights and quotes from your research

For your story to be compelling, it needs to be clear, concise, and engaging. Creating a one-page document or just a couple of slides is usually enough. The key is to present this information "live" to your stakeholders instead of just emailing it around. The passion of your presentation, combined with the hard data you've collected and your empathy towards solving your customer's problem, will get you the buy-in you need.

Let's look at a concrete example of a problem your company might have agreed to explore: "Help customers monitor the health of their equipment."

This statement helped guide your team in establishing an initial direction, but it's not detailed enough to build a potential product. After your research, you discovered you could target the following market:

- **Industry:** renewable energy

- **Company size:** large wind farms (100+ turbines)

- **Geography:** United States

- **Champion:** director of operations

- **Use case:** health monitoring of wind turbines

The target market information provides context and direction, but it is very dry. It is not compelling. By combining this data with the context of the four questions you asked your Champions during your interviews, you have everything you need to craft a compelling story.

Here's an example of what that story could look like:

> Directors of operations responsible for large wind farms in the United States struggle to meet their revenue goals because they lose money when wind turbines break down unexpectedly. This is a serious problem because about ten turbines fail every month. When a turbine goes offline unexpectedly, it takes months for parts to arrive and service to be scheduled. Meanwhile, the turbine is sitting idle, not generating energy and revenue. This problem is particularly costly in off-shore farms where replacement parts can take up to two months to arrive, making the downtime even longer. Wind farm operators lose about $xx per day for every turbine that is not working. They also incur penalties of $yy for not keeping their SLAs with the grid operators. A solution to this problem could save them $zz per year.

This story is impactful because it

- incorporates a clear description of the target market to go after;

- outlines a concrete pain that is keeping your Champion up at night;

- describes the impact of the problem and how much a solution can save the customer;

- gives context on how often the problem occurs and even where the problem is most critical: off-shore wind farms; and

- involves the human element of empathy towards solving your customer's pain.

For additional impact, I recommend reinforcing your story with quotes from your interviews and even photos or videos from your on-site visits. Nothing is more powerful than experiencing the problem yourself or hearing it directly in the voice of the customer.

Your one-pager should also include information about the market size, the companies you talked to, and the potential you see for this opportunity.

Get Buy-In

Once you craft a story, it's time to present it to your Advisory Board. During that meeting, your goal is to convince your audience that this is an excellent opportunity and that you need their support to move to stage three of the B2B Innovator's Map, the User Discovery stage.

On the other hand, if your research shows that your idea doesn't have potential, then the goal of this meeting is to provide an update and propose one of the following options:

- **Option 1:** Iterate on the Market Discovery stage to explore other target markets.

- **Option 2:** Go back to the Strategic Alignment stage to agree on a new customer business outcome to explore.

- **Option 3:** Cancel this initiative altogether.

The key is to keep all your stakeholders in the loop and be transparent with them. Many of the opportunities you research will result in a dead-end. It's essential that your company becomes accustomed to the iterative nature of the process and continues to support exploring other ideas and markets until you find one that has promise.

> **PRO TIP:** When presenting an opportunity to your leadership team, they might agree with the data you are sharing, but they probably have

> questions about what it takes to go from where you are today to the point where you are generating revenue. This is an excellent opportunity to walk your leadership team through the six stages of the B2B Innovator's Map so that they understand where you are and what lies ahead. This also allows you to showcase that your team has the necessary skills (or know-how to get those skills) to navigate each stage of the innovation journey. The balance between showcasing an opportunity and instilling trust that you can execute on that opportunity will gain you the trust and executive support you need.

REAL-WORLD STORY

I remember an eye-opening experience when my team and I interviewed our Champion, Carlos, an operations manager at a mid-sized condominium. Our goal was to understand their challenges around energy consumption. Before this research project, our company believed that our customer spent their day in a pristine control room, looking at big screens mounted on all walls, trying to figure out how to improve the building's energy consumption minute-by-minute. But our on-site visits uncovered a very different reality.

My team and I hoped to arrive at Carlos' facility, step into his office for some coffee, and kickstart the day with a conversation about his top priorities and challenges. Then, he'd give us a tour of his control room, where he'd demonstrate how he monitors his building, and we would end the day back in his office for more coffee, snacks, and whiteboard discussions on how to tackle his challenges. Oh, how wrong we were!

Instead, Carlos greeted us at the front door and asked us to walk with him while we talked. He seemed to be in a rush. "It's a crazy day," he said. "We are doing a renovation in the cafeteria, and we have a couple of water leaks that we need to take care of."

We walked straight into his office, which was nothing like we imagined. Instead of a pristine environment, his office was a small, dark room in the basement. It was full of tools, but not of the digital kind as we had imagined. It was full of construction, garden, and plumbing tools. In the back corner, there was a small desk covered with papers. There was an ancient computer with a monitor from the nineties. And the keyboard was buried under a stack of documents, which meant Carlos didn't spend much time on his computer. Then Carlos moved a hard hat from a dusty chair and grabbed his clipboard. "OK, let's go," he said. "Tell me, what would you like to know?"

As we followed him around the building, we tried to get some of our questions in, but we didn't make much progress. We were interrupted every five minutes by someone from Carlos' staff requiring his attention. "The plumber is here." "The

Market Discovery

catering hasn't arrived." "The tenants from the third floor are complaining again that their air conditioning doesn't work." And so on.

At some point, Carlos turned to us and said, "Yes, reducing my energy bill is important, but I have many other fires to fight every day. To be honest, I just don't have time to monitor my energy bill that closely." My team tried to ask a follow-up question, but we were interrupted again by a security guard saying a homeless person broke into the facility through the back patio. At that moment, Carlos escorted us out of the building and said, "I hope this was helpful and you got the info you were looking for. Sorry, but I need to go."

I could write a whole book about anecdotes like that. During those visits, the information we gathered was invaluable because it clearly showed that our product was not top of mind for our Champion. They needed the value we offered (saving money on their electricity bill), but they didn't have the time or interest to manage it closely. They just wanted the outcome. These visits also gave us a realistic picture of our user's context. The visits gave us clear direction on how to design our product to ensure it was valuable and usable in our customer's environment. For example, this experience helped us update our roadmap to focus less on fancy dashboards (our customers never looked at them) and more on simple alerts. It also made the mobile experience our top priority because our Champions and their staff are always on the move and most likely won't have a "control room" with desktop computers.

Experiences like these are beneficial because you'll have many anecdotes and insights to take back to your company. And although hearing about the stories is powerful, the best outcome is when more people in your company experience the customer's world with you. As you plan on-site visits, make sure you invite people from other departments. On-site visits are an excellent opportunity to bring your extended team closer together and for everybody to experience the customer's pain firsthand.

If you have agreement on the target market to pursue, and you have a clear understanding of who your Champion is and what their pains are, then congratulations! You completed the Market Discovery stage of the innovation journey. You should be very proud. Take a moment to celebrate with your team. This is a big milestone.

Although you have a lot of work ahead of you, you are already ahead of most companies, since very few take the time to complete this stage. By completing this work, you have set your team and your company on the path to success.

Once you are done with that celebration, it's time to move to stage three of the innovation journey: the User Discovery stage! See you there.

Learn More

By becoming familiar with the Market Discovery process, you will feel comfortable giving direction to your team, and you'll have the know-how to sell the value of discovery inside your organization. Below you'll find a few of my favorite books to help you dive deeper into the mechanics of leveraging customer interactions to unearth opportunities:

- *Lean Customer Development: Building Products Your Customers Will Buy* by Cindy Alvarez

- *Continuous Discovery Habits: Discover Products that Create Customer Value and Business Value* by Teresa Torres

- *The Mom Test: How to Talk to Customers and Learn If Your Business Is a Good Idea When Everyone Is Lying to You* by Rob Fitzpatrick

- *The Four Steps to the Epiphany: Successful Strategies for Products that Win* by Steve Blank

Note: *For an extended list of books, the companion workbook, and additional resources, download your B2B Innovator's Kit at https://danielelizalde.com/b2b-innovators-kit.*

User Discovery

NOTHING IS AS POWERFUL AS EXPERIENCING YOUR CUSTOMER'S pains firsthand.

Early in my career, I worked for a large industrial automation company. I was part of a new consulting team focused on building end-to-end solutions using the company's software and hardware. It was a fantastic opportunity to work onsite with our customers and get immersed in their world.

I had the opportunity to work at a high-speed mobile phone manufacturing plant in Finland, a diamond-sorting mine in South Africa, inside the Linear Accelerator at Stanford University, at a facility testing micro-turbines for decentralized energy production, and many other incredible applications. Regardless of how "exotic" these assignments were, the most significant learning was just being there with the customer, experiencing their problems through their own eyes.

I loved sharing my customer findings with the engineering team, but to my surprise, these insights were not well received. I often heard that my findings were just outliers or that the customers didn't know what they needed. As it often happens in B2B companies, our product roadmap was not based on any customer evidence. It was based on what the engineering team thought the customer needed, or from what they heard from a couple of sales folks.

It took several months, but as I continued bringing more and more customer feedback, I started gaining the trust of my engineering team. And that's when the breakthroughs started to happen. During a visit to a high-volume contract manufacturer, I learned about their need to improve their manufacturing yields without buying more hardware. I'd heard that pain multiple times, so that evening, I wrote a small software prototype to solve the problem and presented it to the customer. They loved it, and so did a few other customers.

I was excited to share my findings with my engineering team. They realized this feature wasn't in their roadmap, but given the customer evidence I had, they understood this feature solved a real pain and that it would be very valuable to many customers. Therefore, they agreed to productize my algorithm and incorporate it into the software. That feature was a big hit! We received a patent for it, and even today, years after this story, that feature is one of the top three best-selling features of the product.

User Discovery

The point of this story is that you can't guess what your customer needs, and you can't dream up solutions in a room and hope they solve a problem that a customer doesn't have. Working closely with your users to understand their pains *and* working with your engineering team to find solutions to those pains is the root of all innovation.

Now, I must say that, at that time, I didn't have the necessary tools to get the best insights from customer interactions or the techniques to analyze the data I gathered. I did everything based on "gut feeling" and trial and error. But you don't have to. In this chapter, I share with you the blueprint on how to engage with your users, analyze the data, and incorporate those insights into your solution.

In the Market Discovery stage, you identified a target market to explore, verified the market's size, and engaged with the Champion in that target market to understand their pains. If you were building a consumer product, this information would be enough to start iterating on a solution. But in the world of enterprise software, you need to go one level deeper. You need to identify all the people supporting the Champion in achieving the desired business outcome. I call this group of people your User Ecosystem.

In Chapter 1, I mentioned that understanding enterprise customers means understanding the company's desired business outcome and the people, processes, and tools involved in achieving that outcome. Your User Ecosystem represents the people who follow a process set by the Champion to achieve a business outcome. Your product is the tool that supports those people along the process and, as a result, helps your Champion achieve their goal.

On the journey between idea and your first ten customers, you are here:

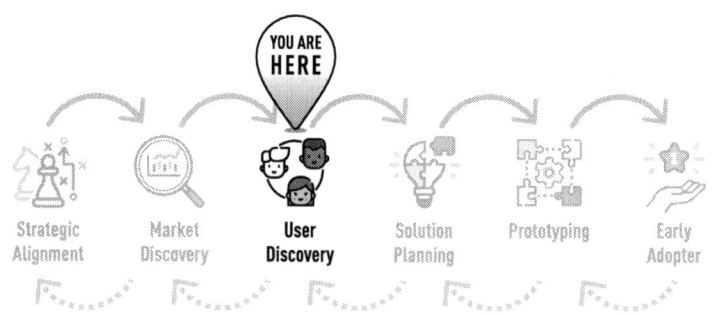

Understanding your User Ecosystem goes deeper than knowing who those people are. It requires understanding their pains, motivations, and workflows within the Champion's process. I divide the problem of understanding your User Ecosystem into two parts:

1. Discover all the users in your ecosystem.

2. Research your User Ecosystem's pains and opportunities.

User Discovery

During the User Discovery stage, you might discover that your User Ecosystem has just a handful of users, or you might realize it has dozens (which is not rare for enterprise software). At this stage, focus on identifying and understanding *all* the people in the User Ecosystem. Don't worry if you find too many and it looks like an unmanageable situation. In stage four of the B2B Innovator's Map (Solution Planning), you will prioritize which users to focus on for your first ten customers.

DISCOVER ALL THE USERS IN YOUR ECOSYSTEM

The best way to discover all the users in your ecosystem is to talk to your Champion so you can understand the process, tools, and people involved in achieving the desired outcome. Let's look at an example of how you can obtain this information.

Let's assume that you work for a company building enterprise eCommerce solutions. During the Market Discovery stage, you identified the chief marketing officer (CMO) at a toy manufacturer as your Champion. Their desired business outcome is to improve online sales, but they struggle with the complexity and lack of flexibility of their existing eCommerce tools. Your conversation could go something like this:

You: Could you walk me through your process for offering a new toy on your website? What are the steps, what systems do you use, and who is involved?

CMO: The head of manufacturing notifies the marketing team that a new toy is available to sell. Then the director of marketing works with his team to take photos of the toy, write the toy's description, and upload it to our digital catalog. Then Peter, the merchandising manager, sets up a few discount coupons as part of the launch, and then he publishes the item on our website. When a shopper orders the toy online, our inventory manager gets an email with the order details. The toy is packaged and sent to the shopper, who can track the shipment on our website. Our retail analyst generates a sales report at the end of the month, including online and physical stores. That report makes it to our quarterly executive meeting, where I review the data with my peers and make adjustments for the next quarter.

You will need to ask more probing questions to get this level of detail, but from this story, you've learned that at least seven people are involved in this process:

- CMO (the Champion)
- Head of manufacturing
- Director of marketing
- Merchandising manager
- Your customer's shopper
- Inventory manager
- Retail analyst

User Discovery

> **PRO TIP:** Different companies can have different titles for the same function. Ensure your team focuses on discovering the "roles" that the various people play, instead of just the titles.

After talking with Champions from multiple companies, you will get a clear picture of the people and processes involved in delivering the desired business outcome. Later, you'll need to dive deeper into each of those users' pains to uncover opportunities where your product can make a difference. For now, let's focus on making sure you've identified *all* the potential users in the ecosystem across the enterprise customer lifecycle. This includes people within your customer's organization, partners, and people within your own organization.

Discovering all users means you'll dive into these four areas:

1. Users across the enterprise customer lifecycle

2. Partners and vendors in the ecosystem

3. Users internal to your organization

4. Users involved in compliance

Discover Users Across the Enterprise Customer Lifecycle

All B2B software goes through the seven phases of the enterprise customer lifecycle:

1. Evaluation and Purchase

2. Installation

3. Deployment

4. Onboarding

5. Operations

6. Maintenance

7. Decommission

The example about the toy manufacturer revealed seven critical roles involved in delivering the company's desired outcome. One thing those users have in common is that they are all working in the "Operations" phase of the enterprise customer lifecycle. In other words, the users can access your product because your product has already been installed, deployed, and configured for that customer.

When delivering value to your first ten customers, most of your efforts will revolve around solving the users' pains in the

User Discovery

Operations phase. But it is vital to understand the people and processes throughout the complete enterprise customer lifecycle because:

- Your Champion will want to know the details on how you'll deploy your solution.

- Once an early customer buys your solution, your team will need to go through various phases of the customer lifecycle before arriving at the Operations phase. So it's essential to know what lies ahead.

- Depending on your industry, early phases such as Installation and Deployment can be lengthy, expensive, and burdensome with regulation. The more you know now, the better prepared you will be.

- Eventually, your product will need features to support all users across the enterprise customer lifecycle phases. By understanding all stakeholders and workflows across the lifecycle, you can start planning for any necessary features you might need to build later.

- Sometimes, the user with the most significant pain is outside the Operations phase. For example, enterprise software is known for taking a long time to deploy. If your product reduces deployment time and cost, then you'll have a significant value proposition for your Champion.

Discovering the User Ecosystem across the enterprise customer lifecycle follows the same approach you learned earlier in this chapter. Simply ask your Champion to describe the process and people involved at each phase of the enterprise customer lifecycle.

Let's look at each phase of the enterprise customer lifecycle in more detail.

1. Evaluation and Purchase

Enterprise products follow a B2B sales model, requiring your customer's buying committee to evaluate the potential value of your solution before making a purchasing decision. This is true even if you are only selling a pilot program for your first ten customers. That's why it's critical to understand who is involved in the Evaluation and Purchase phase, who is the decision-maker, and what they need to see before closing the deal. In addition to sales demos and sandboxes, you might discover that the gatekeeper is IT (or other departments), and you'll need to incorporate features to meet their needs if you want to be considered for a pilot program.

2. Installation

If your company sells a cloud-based product, then the Installation phase might be seamless for your customer. But if your product has an "on-premise" option or includes a

User Discovery

combination of software and hardware, the installation can be very complex, expensive, and time-consuming. For most enterprise software products, a typical user in this phase is your customer's IT department and people from the cybersecurity and compliance departments. If you are selling an industrial product, your users might also include people in OT and even system integrators.

3. Deployment

Enterprise software products often need a Deployment phase to get them working for the specific needs of your customers. I'm using "deployment" as the umbrella term for all the different activities your team needs to complete to get your product ready to use. The Deployment phase includes data migration, integration with legacy and third-party systems, configuration, and even customization. Your product might need to expose application programming interfaces (APIs) or provide utilities for migration and configuration to meet those needs. It is crucial to understand who needs to interact with these APIs and utilities so your product can offer the right toolset for the right people. I've seen many pilot programs die because the Deployment phase took too long, was too complex, or was too expensive. You don't want to burn any bridges with your first ten customers, so the more you learn about their deployment requirements, the better your solution will be.

For your first ten customers, your internal engineering team will likely conduct any deployment activities. This is an excellent opportunity to learn what is required during the Deployment phase so that your team can develop tools for your customers or partners to perform these deployments in the future.

4. Onboarding

It is not uncommon for companies to buy and install new products that they never use. To avoid this fate and to ensure your product will deliver on its promise, make sure you plan how you'll onboard and train your User Ecosystem within each of your first ten customers. Your goal is to understand the onboarding needs of your User Ecosystem, including supporting functions such as IT, OT, and support teams. Once your product matures, onboarding will be taken over by your customer success team, but that comes much later. At this early stage, your innovation team needs to work closely with your first ten customers to onboard everybody in the User Ecosystem and ensure they are getting the value you promised.

5. Operations

As I mentioned earlier, the Operations phase is where your customer finally starts getting value out of your product because it's where the day-to-day usage of your product occurs. Your goal is to understand who interacts with your product daily and how your product can support their critical workflows.

6. Maintenance

During the Maintenance phase, your goal is to identify who is involved in maintaining your product and what features they need to anticipate failures, troubleshoot them, and repair them. These features will be different depending on who performs the maintenance. Some companies have internal maintenance teams. Others look at the product vendor to provide that maintenance, and yet others hire external companies, such as system integration companies, to provide maintenance. Understanding how your target market deals with maintenance will inform your roadmap and can open the door for new revenue opportunities for your company to offer maintenance services.

7. Decommission

In a worst-case scenario, your customer might decide to cancel your contract and ask to decommission your product. Maybe your product didn't deliver on its promise. Perhaps your customer chose to go with your competition. Or maybe your customer's business changed, and they don't need your product anymore. Regardless of the reason, your team needs to understand what is involved in decommissioning your product and who is involved in that process.

When negotiating a pilot project with your first ten customers, each customer will want to know the details on how you handle contract cancellations. For example, what happens with their data, how long will it take to remove access to the system and shut it down, how will you remove any physical devices you installed, etc. Having answers to these questions will give your Champion the confidence to try out your product. Your Champion will understand that, if you cannot deliver on the value you promised, at least you'll be able to decommission your product so both parties can move on quickly.

Discover Partners and Vendors in the Ecosystem

As you talk to people in your target market, pay attention to whether your customer outsources any part of their process to external vendors or partners. Understanding your User Ecosystem includes understanding the involvement of these third-party companies who support your customer's business outcome.

Depending on your industry, the participation of third parties might be small, or it might play a critical role. For example, in the manufacturing industry, it is common for Champions to rely on system integrators to make purchasing decisions and provide the deployment and integration of automation solutions. In this manufacturing scenario, your actual user during the Evaluation and Purchase, Installation, and Deployment phases of the lifecycle is often somebody working for the system integration company. Therefore, you need to make sure your product solves their needs, such as ease of installation, compatibility with other systems, flexibility of customization, etc.

User Discovery

When working with your first ten customers, you might need to interact with some of those third-party vendors, so it's essential for your team to understand who they are and their role in supporting your customers' business outcomes.

Discover Users Internal to Your Organization

In addition to discovering all the users on your customer's side, it is essential to understand any potential users from within your organization. These internal users will require internal tools to install and deploy the system, check compliance, analyze data, provide maintenance, etc.

Early in the innovation journey, it is likely that all of your internal users will be part of your engineering and product teams. That's because it's too early to start involving other groups and because your team needs to experience firsthand the pains of installing, deploying, and operating your product. Those learnings will be invaluable beyond your first ten customers when it's time to start optimizing for scale.

To discover your internal users, I recommend walking through the enterprise customer lifecycle with your team and asking the question, "Based on what we know from our Champion and the User Ecosystem, who, from within our company, needs to be involved during each phase of the customer lifecycle?"

This question opens up discussions on who, from within your company, should be involved during Evaluation, Installation,

Operations, etc. Just like with your external users, when I say "who," I'm not referring to a specific person. Instead, you are looking for the role of the person who will perform that function.

Understanding your internal users will give you an early preview of what it will take to deploy and operate this new product. A map of your internal users will also be invaluable information as you make the business case (i.e., the cost associated with operating your product) to your executive team to move forward with this initiative.

Discover Users Involved in Compliance

Complying with rules and regulations is an important part of building B2B products. Regulatory compliance doesn't have to be an obscure and daunting subject. Look, I'm not saying it is fun and exciting, but with a little bit of reframing, you can make it manageable and predictable.

Instead of thinking of regulations as something abstract you need to comply with, think of it in terms of users and their needs. Remember, as an Innovator, everything you do revolves around solving the needs of people. Therefore, instead of thinking about the regulations themselves, think about the people involved in the compliance process. And therefore, think of those people as additional users in your User Ecosystem. Those users are an important part of the success of your product, and they have genuine needs that you can help them solve.

For example, if you are building accounting software, and one of your customers is audited by the government, ask yourself: How can my product make it easy for my customer to comply with the audit? What functionality do I need to expose? What data should I make available to the government auditor? In this scenario, both the government auditor and your customer's compliance team are the users you need to solve for.

Here's another example from the renewable energy industry. Let's say you sell control software for solar panels for commercial buildings. Before your customer can operate their new solar panels, an inspector needs to review the installation to ensure everything is up to code. In this scenario, you can ask yourself: What data does the inspector need to see to certify the system? How can I make it easy for my customers and inspectors to collaborate to expedite the approval of a new solar deployment?

The key is to look past the regulation itself and focus on discovering the people (and their needs) involved in complying with that regulation across the enterprise customer lifecycle.

Organize All the Information About Your User Ecosystem

After conducting several interviews with Champions in multiple companies, you will have the necessary information to map your User Ecosystem. The next step is to synthesize all this information, prioritize it, and plan for the next steps.

The most efficient way to perform this synthesis is to do it as an in-person or virtual workshop. The goal of the workshop is to summarize all the types of users your team discovered by talking to multiple Champions. The goal right now is only to identify all the users. Don't worry if you don't have all the information about the pains of each user. You'll get to that part later in this chapter.

To prepare for the workshop:

- Schedule a working session with your team. Consider inviting a few key stakeholders who are interested in being more hands-on during this process. This will continue to build rapport and trust with key people in the organization.

- In preparation for the meeting, ask the people who conducted the Champion interviews to write down on individual sticky notes the role or title of all potential users they discovered.

- On a whiteboard (virtual or in-person), create a table with seven columns and four rows.

    * Label the columns using the seven phases of the enterprise customer lifecycle.

    * Label the first row "Customer," second row "Partner," third row "Internal," and last row "Compliance." Here is what the table would look like:

User Discovery

	Evaluate and Purchase	Installation	Deployment	Onboarding	Operations	Maintenance	Decommission
Customer							
Partner							
Internal							
Compliance							

To run the workshop:

- Start the meeting by reminding everybody that you are in the User Discovery stage of the innovation journey. The goal of this workshop is to review your Champion interviews and generate a list of all the potential users in your ecosystem.

- Start the exercise by asking the people who conducted the interviews to place their sticky notes on the corresponding column and row. Ask each person to give a brief (ten seconds) description of each user they discovered.

    * Group sticky notes of users that perform the same function, even if they have different titles.

    * If a particular role is involved during multiple enterprise customer lifecycle phases, add them to all the appropriate phases.

- Once all sticky notes are on the whiteboard, facilitate discussion on how to group similar roles into a single role, which you'll use moving forward.

  * For example, let's say that each company you talked to uses a different title for the person performing the same function during the Operations phase. In this case, keep the title that makes the most sense for your team.

- Finally, ask your team, "Are we missing any user across the lifecycle?"

Once you complete this table, it will represent the first holistic view of your User Ecosystem. Seeing this table for the first time can be daunting because of the number of users involved and the anticipation of how much software you'll need to build. Don't worry. In the Solution Planning stage, you will prioritize which users to tackle first and focus on delivering only what is needed to provide value to your first ten customers.

Your next step is to dive deeper into each of the users in your ecosystem to understand their pains and their role in supporting your Champion's business outcome.

RESEARCH YOUR USER ECOSYSTEM'S PAINS AND OPPORTUNITIES

Now that you've identified your User Ecosystem, your next step is to dive deeper into the users' needs to understand how they perform their work today and which issues you could potentially solve for them. Remember that the Champion is responsible for the overall business outcome and leads the process to achieve that goal. But the people in your User Ecosystem are the ones who will use your product to improve some aspect of that process. By understanding the pains of the individual users, you can uncover the biggest hurdles for achieving the business outcome. If you can provide a product that makes that portion of the process more efficient, then you'll have a very valuable proposition for your Champion.

The Champions are usually responsible for the end-to-end process to achieve the business outcome. But that doesn't mean that your product needs to support the complete end-to-end operation. Maybe as your product gains traction in this market, you can continue to expand it, but you don't have to start there. You can begin by supporting just a tiny portion of the process, as long as your approach results in a better/faster/cheaper way to get to the desired outcome.

For example, let's say your Champion is an SVP of Sales looking to improve the visibility of his sales pipeline. Your first inclination might be to tackle the complete sales process with a CRM-type product. But that might not be what your target market needs. They might be happy with their current CRM but struggle only with the analysis and visibility of the sales pipeline. Therefore, your opportunity in this market might be to create a new product that integrates with existing CRM solutions and optimizes the visibility into that pipeline. In this case, you would focus only on a partial set of users from the overall CRM User Ecosystem, but you'd be more focused, and you would have a better chance to deliver something of value.

On the other hand, there might be situations where you can provide a better solution for the end-to-end problem. Ideally, your product would provide a superior solution for every user in the ecosystem, but that might not be realistic, especially this early in your product journey. Instead, your team should focus on providing the basic functionality your User Ecosystem expects and concentrate on delivering a superior experience for one or two of the users. Continuing with the CRM example, this means your product would provide the core functionality an enterprise expects from a CRM (i.e., "table stakes" functionality), *and* you'd include several differentiated features that would set your product apart.

Whether you plan to deliver a solution for an end-to-end process or plan to focus on a specific area, the key to knowing which product to build will emerge from diving deeper into the User Ecosystem's needs.

User Discovery

Dig Deeper into the Needs of Your User Ecosystem

Your goal is to understand the process of each of the users in the ecosystem, including their goals, the steps they take, the tools they use today, and the main challenges they face.

Once again, on-site visits and user interviews are the most powerful tools to quickly understand your users. For each user type, you can gather insights by asking open-ended questions, including:

- Can you describe/draw your process for doing X?

- What does your typical workday look like?

- Which tools do you use today (digital or otherwise) to support this process?

- What are you not able to do today with your current tools/process?

- What are the parts of the process that take the most time/are the most difficult? Why?

- If you could use magic to change anything in this area automatically, what would that be?

With so many users in an ecosystem, scheduling eight to twelve interviews with each type of user can quickly bubble up to hundreds of interviews. This can be daunting and can take a long time. I recommend talking to all the types of users you've identified, but you can do it on a smaller scale. Plan to interview two to three people of each user type. Then double down on interviews for the roles where you can deliver the most value or that have expressed the most considerable pain. That way, you'll get good coverage and customer-driven insights, but you won't spend all your time and resources just doing research.

> **PRO TIP:** You will know you can stop interviewing new users when you notice a convergence of pains across many interviews and you see that additional interviews don't deliver any new insights.

As your team conducts all these interviews, you'll need a way to organize all the information and synthesize the customer insights so you can use them to drive the following stages of the journey. The best approach is to synthesize all your customer information into personas.

Create Personas of Your Champion and Your User Ecosystem

Now that you collected all this information about your users, how do you use it to move forward?

User Discovery

The information about your users' pains will help you in two areas:

- To convey to your company who your users are and what their pains are.

- To anchor every design, business, and technology decision around the needs of your customers.

I'm a strong advocate of using Alan Cooper's "personas" to capture and communicate your customer's insights. **I define a persona, also known as an avatar, simply as the representation of your ideal user.** It's critical to understand that a persona is not a real person. It's just a representation of all the characteristics of your ideal users and customers. I say this because I work with many companies who create personas based on their best (or only) customers. This is a trap because it assumes that your target audience is just like your only customer, which is often not the case.

Also, keep in mind that you will need to build a persona for each user you have discovered in your ecosystem. If your solution has ten users, then you'll need to draft ten unique personas. As you go through this exercise with your team, you might realize that, for the sake of making product decisions, you can combine a few personas, or, in many cases, you might realize you are missing some other users that also need a persona. In the Solution Planning stage, you'll prioritize which personas to go after, so at this point, don't worry if you are faced with a lot of personas. At this stage, the most important thing is to document all potential users in your ecosystem.

If you are new to the concept of personas, it is easy to get overwhelmed. Don't be. At its core, a persona is just a document that describes the key characteristics of your user. To create a persona, you simply need to synthesize the feedback you gathered from talking to many users into a cohesive document. The exact content and format of the persona document will vary across companies. Just make sure that every item you include in the persona helps you understand your users and helps you make decisions about the direction of your product. It is also helpful to include other people in the persona creation process. UX Designers in particular are likely to have experience building personas and can bring a lot of value to the process.

The elements I recommend including in a persona are:

- **Photo:** Stock photo or any headshot of a person that fits the description of your user. The goal is to "humanize" the persona, and that's a lot easier to do if you have a photo representing that user.

- **Name and title:** A fictitious name and the most common title you've identified for this person (e.g., VP of Operations, Field Engineer). You can also add additional titles if you discovered that this user might have a different title in different companies.

- **Years of experience in this role:** I include this as proxy information for whether you'll need to build a product for a beginner or an expert user.

- **Core need(s):** A few bullet points of the pains that keep this person up at night. Ideally, their pains are related to the problem you are trying to solve, but they don't have to be. It is essential to recognize that some of these users have a pain that's just tangential to your solution, but you need to consider them as part of your User Ecosystem.

- **Quote:** Add a quote you heard during your interviews. This continues to humanize your user and makes the pain more tangible.

Here's an example persona. As you can see, the format is simple to read, and it's not overwhelming. It makes for a great internal communication tool you can share with your product team, Advisory Board, and leadership teams.

James Price, 35

Wind Turbine Service Technician

10 years of experience

"My average day is spent climbing and inspecting multiple turbines."

James' Needs:

- Monitor health of my wind farm, and look into problems with specific turbines
- Schedule and manage maintenance for each turbine that needs service
- Report health status of the farm quarterly to my boss

Personas are an alignment and decision-making tool, so you should avoid adding information that is just fluff and will not help you make product decisions.

I often see personas include information like gender, age, brand affinity, nationality, hobbies, number of children, etc. Adding this information might give you the feeling of "knowing your user," but in reality, it is just another form of innovation theater. Every field in your persona must help you make evidence-based product decisions. Unless you plan to develop a different solution based on gender, age, or brand affinity, I recommend keeping such items out of your persona, since they just add to the noise.

User Discovery

UNCOVER THE OPPORTUNITIES TO FOCUS ON

Let's take a minute to recap all the work you've done so far:

- You talked to many Champions to understand who is involved in their process.

- You used that information to map your User Ecosystem across the enterprise customer lifecycle and the various types of users.

- You researched your user's pains.

- You created user personas.

That's a lot of work! Congratulations. This work is the foundation for everything else you need to accomplish throughout the innovation journey.

Now it's time to dive into these insights to uncover opportunities for you to improve the lives of your users and help your Champion achieve their goals.

To uncover those opportunities, work with your team to evaluate all the user insights you have and answer these four questions:

1. Are there any users with significant pains or underserved needs?

2. Will solving the needs of the user(s) help the Champion achieve their goal more efficiently, or will it just result in benefits for that user without impacting the overarching business goal?

3. Is there an opportunity for our team to provide an innovative and differentiated solution to that pain?

4. Are those pains within the boundaries of the pain we agreed to explore during the Strategic Alignment stage?

At this stage, focus only on whether you have an opportunity or not. Don't worry about *how* you will implement a solution since that's the focus of the following three stages of the B2B Innovator's Map. For now, your goal is to identify potential opportunities your company can focus on. Once you have the answers to the questions above, it's time to get together with your Advisory Board and discuss the next steps.

ALIGNMENT AND NEXT STEPS

Now that you uncovered some exciting opportunities to help your users, it's time to meet with your Advisory Board to discuss your next steps. Here's what you need to cover with your Advisory Board:

- Provide them context reiterating you are on stage three (User Discovery) of a six-stage journey.

User Discovery

- Revisit the agreements you already made, including the agreement on the problem to explore (from the Strategic Alignment stage) and the target market to go after (from the Market Discovery stage).

- Share your findings around the User Ecosystem. Include interview quotes, share the table with the User Ecosystem you mapped out, and showcase the personas you created.

- Once everybody digests the new insights, it's time to propose the next steps.

Your proposed next step will fall into two categories:

- If you've identified the critical users with severe pains your company could solve, then your proposed next steps should be to move forward to the Solution Planning stage in the B2B Innovator's Map (stage four).

- If you haven't identified strong opportunities your company could address with a new product, then you can propose one of these three options:

    * **Option 1:** Spend more time on the User Discovery stage talking to other users in the ecosystem.

* **Option 2:** Go back to the Market Discovery stage and explore a different target market.

* **Option 3:** Go back to the Strategic Alignment stage to agree on a different customer business outcome to explore.

REAL-WORLD STORY

Years ago, I worked as Director of Programs at a UX agency specializing in user-centered design. At the time, mobile phones and tablets were starting to take the market by storm. There was a rush for every application to "go mobile," so the CEO of an accounting software company hired our agency to define what their mobile experience should look like.

To guide the design direction, the project included a user research phase to understand the users' workflow and daily activities. The CEO was reluctant to take this step because he wanted to jump directly into the user interface design. In his mind, he knew what customers needed, so it was just a matter of crafting his vision on a mobile device. He finally agreed to a short user research project, but his expectations were very low.

The CEO's target market was medium-size accounting firms. And the core users were accountants responsible for managing their clients' books and tax preparation. Visiting a few of these accounting firms and understanding the way they work

User Discovery

was very eye-opening. My team conducted a few onsite interviews and created some quick prototypes to test key workflows. The results were unexpected, at least for the CEO.

It turns out that accountants didn't see a need for a mobile version of the software since they spend all of their days at their desks. There wasn't a need to continue working on the go. The paper prototypes my team created also uncovered that the workflows and data entry requirements would be hard to reproduce without a mouse and keyboard. They saw a mobile version as hampering their productivity instead of increasing it. In short, there was no desirable use case for a mobile version of the software.

We knew that delivering this news to the CEO would be explosive. He hired us to do a job, and instead, we came back to tell him that his idea had no future. During the meeting, the CEO was not happy at all. Anticipating his reaction, we compiled a list of opportunities we discovered during the on-site interviews. We heard many statements like "We don't need a mobile version, but if you could fix this other part of the process, that'd be very valuable." This list of opportunities resonated well with the CEO's goals. After all, creating a mobile experience was only a means to an end. The desired business outcome was to increase his product's differentiation, and therefore, if those new opportunities would help him get there, the whole effort would be successful.

The takeaway from this story is that User Discovery is a tool to increase your chances of success. Without this short

THE B2B INNOVATOR'S MAP

discovery effort, the CEO would have spent millions of dollars and many months developing a mobile solution that nobody wanted. Given the hype and fast-growing trend of mobile adoption, it made sense to think that everything needed to be mobile. But that was not the case. The key is to work closely with your users to understand their workflows and how your tools can help them be more effective at their job.

Don't be discouraged if you are not able to move to the Solution Planning stage immediately. It will take a few iterations before you find enough customer evidence to proceed to stage four. With every iteration, you build momentum with your customers and continue building trust within your organization. Keep doing the work. You are on the right track!

Learn More

Here are some of my favorite books to dive deeper into the strategies and tactics of understanding your users' pains:

- *Jobs to Be Done: Theory to Practice* by Tony Ulwick

- *Product Research Rules: Nine Foundational Rules for Product Teams to Run Accurate Research that Delivers Actionable Insight by C.* Todd Lombardo and Aras Bilgen

User Discovery

- *Interviewing Users: How to Uncover Compelling Insights* by Steve Portigal

Note: *Get an extended list of books, the companion workbook, and additional resources by downloading your B2B Innovator's Kit at https://danielelizalde.com/b2b-innovators-kit.*

CHAPTER 5

Solution Planning

A FEW YEARS BACK, I STARTED WORKING WITH A COMPANY building a new enterprise eCommerce platform. However, as I started engaging with the team, I had a hard time visualizing what they were building. I talked to more people in the organization and realized that everybody had a different mental vision of the product and its components.

The goal of the Solution Planning stage is to align your teams on how you will approach the iterative process of testing and developing your solution. It is an opportunity to step back, look at all the progress you've made so far, and get ready for the road ahead.

Stages one through three of the B2B Innovator's Map focus on learning about your customer to minimize the risk of building a product nobody wants. But once you have enough customer insights and the backing from your company to pursue an opportunity, you can't be focused 100 percent on learning anymore. You need to switch your focus to a more balanced approach of learning and building.

Stages four through six of the B2B Innovator's Map focus on iteratively testing and building a solution that will (hopefully) address your customer's needs. You are currently here:

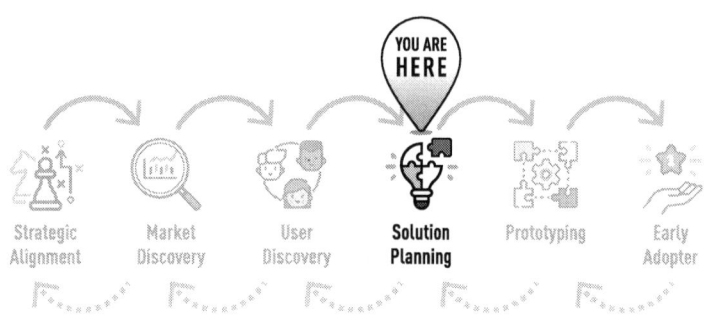

The Solution Planning stage takes less time to complete than other stages since all you'll need is a handful of working sessions with your team and your Advisory Board. But even though you might complete this stage in just a couple of weeks, don't underestimate its importance. **Getting alignment and buy-in from your leadership team is essential as you move towards your first ten customers.** As many Innovators will tell you, getting the initial buy-in from leadership is easy. Retaining their support during later stages of the innovation journey is the hard part.

Solution Planning

Here are the four steps you need to complete in the Solution Planning stage:

1. Prioritize users

2. Create a Solution Diagram

3. Create an experiment roadmap

4. Get stakeholder alignment and buy-in

Let's look at each of these areas in more detail.

PRIORITIZE USERS

During the User Discovery stage, you gained a robust understanding of your User Ecosystem. The challenge is that you might have discovered ten, fifteen, or more users across the enterprise customer lifecycle, and developing software that meets everyone's needs seems like a herculean task.

Discovering all these users doesn't mean you need to solve their needs—at least not right away. Instead, you should focus on the few users who have the most significant pains. Solving these users' pains will have a substantial impact on achieving the business outcome of your Champion. Also, by focusing on the specific pains of just one or two users, you have the opportunity to create a unique and differentiated product that catches the interest of your Champion and opens the door to your first pilot customer.

To illustrate this point, let's go back to the CRM example from the previous chapter. In that example, the SVP of Sales (the Champion) was responsible for improving the visibility into the sales pipeline. From researching the User Ecosystem, you discovered that the users with the most significant pain were business analysts, because they struggle to put together meaningful reports for the sales leaders. Let's assume your company could provide a solution that better collects, organizes, and displays sales data. In that case, you'd be solving the pains of the business analyst, *and* you would have a significant impact on the Champion's goal. In this scenario, prioritizing a single user results in a lot of value for your Champion.

Compare this approach with what most enterprise companies do. Usually, companies would skip the research portion and try to address the needs of *all* users by developing a complete CRM solution. Each user in the ecosystem would get enhancements here and there but nothing of real value to convince the Champion to abandon their existing solution in place of the new one. From the Champion's perspective, there is not enough value in switching to a whole new CRM unless it provides key visibility enhancements to the sales pipeline (his core pain). Switching to a brand-new CRM becomes a much bigger proposition than just adopting a new module on top of an existing CRM. Adopting a new CRM also involves more significant entry barriers regarding cost, deployment, data migration, configuration, and training.

Solution Planning

Asking companies to switch enterprise solutions is a tricky proposition. But it's even more complicated if the product is brand-new and untested. Your company is more likely to get a foot in the door with a much smaller product that serves only one or two key users. This more specific product can be developed and tested in just a few weeks. Then, as your product evolves to support other areas of your Champion's process, it will be easier for your customer to adopt any new features you develop.

Although the few users you prioritize will most likely be in the Operations phase (since that's the value-generating phase), never lose track of other users throughout the enterprise customer lifecycle. Key users (such as IT) will have requirements in phases outside the Operations phase. Not paying attention to those requirements can be a deal-breaker to move forward even with a pilot project.

In summary, work with your team to analyze your User Ecosystem and come to an agreement about which users (and pains) you should focus on first. Later, during the Prototyping stage, you'll start iteratively testing and building a solution for those user(s), but know that nothing is set in stone. As you continue to iterate, you'll gain more insights. Then you can decide whether you need to increase the scope to include other users or even switch users altogether. The benefit of working in small, iterative chunks is that you have the flexibility to move forward only if you have enough customer insights to verify that you are moving in the right direction.

CREATE A SOLUTION DIAGRAM

Trying to understand the vision for a new enterprise product often feels like the parable of the six blind men and the elephant. In the story, six blind men are placed next to an elephant and are asked to describe what the elephant looks like just by touching the elephant's part closest to them. The man holding the trunk said that an elephant looks like a snake! The man touching a leg said it looks like a tree. The man touching the tail said it must look like a rope. The man holding the elephant's ear said it must look like a rug. And so on.

Most Innovators underestimate how difficult it is to communicate what they plan to build within their organization. People across your organization will have a hard time understanding the overall vision of your product because they lack context or are looking at the new product through their own lens (i.e., engineering, sales, marketing).

Many executives I talk to complain that they don't understand what their teams are creating, so it's hard to continue backing the innovation teams during these critical months of early development. To avoid this fate, before you start testing and building your solution, ensure you have alignment inside your company on what you propose to develop.

Creating a simple Solution Diagram of your proposed product is the best way to get everybody aligned. During my workshops, it's fun to see the light bulb going on in people's faces when they see their product drawn as a simple diagram. I

Solution Planning

often get comments like, "I didn't know that's what we were building" or "That's not at all what I was thinking."

To create a Solution Diagram, simply draw each component of your solution and connect them using lines and arrows to show their relationship. Don't worry, you don't need to be an artist to do this. If you can draw boxes, circles, lines, and arrows, then you can create a Solution Diagram.

Keep in mind this is not an engineering diagram, meaning it doesn't need to represent the nuts and bolts of the solution. Also, it doesn't need to be 100 percent accurate. As long as it depicts the main components of your solution *from a customer perspective*, that's all you need.

> **PRO TIP:** Remember that this diagram is just a communication tool, and it does not represent a team's commitment to building everything you draw in the diagram. Make sure to set this expectation because your leadership team might take your diagram as an actual proposal of what you plan to build. You are not there yet. The pieces you'll build will depend on the results of the tests you conduct in the Prototyping stage. And as you get more customer evidence, you'll update the Solution Diagram to reflect what the actual product will include.

THE B2B INNOVATOR'S MAP

When I was working with the company building a new enterprise eCommerce platform, I created a rough diagram that enabled me to start conversations and get alignment across all departments. The diagram I put together looked something like this:

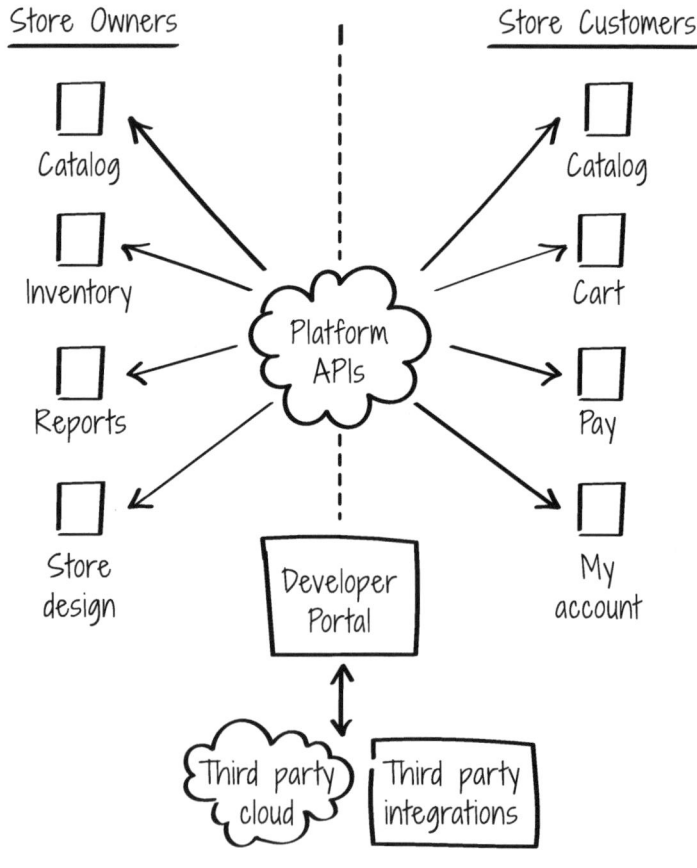

Solution Planning

Notice that my diagram focuses on the components relevant to the users, not to the internal engineering team. With this simple diagram, I was able to clarify the various components of the product, which opened the door to conversations on critical architectural issues. One of the value propositions of this platform was that customers would get an all-in-one solution and didn't need any additional tools to manage their eCommerce store at scale.

When I discussed this drawing with our chief architect, he corrected the part at the bottom. Initially, I'd drawn the arrow of all third-party applications going into our cloud. He took a quick look and corrected it, saying we won't host third-party applications in our cloud. Instead, third-party developers were responsible for hosting their own applications. That might seem like a small detail, but it had enormous repercussions. With this new clarity on how the solution was intended to work, I collaborated with multiple departments to refine the third-party user experience, redefined the positioning for working with third-party developers, and created enablement tools to better demonstrate the system's capabilities.

> **PRO TIP:** A Solution Diagram has no value by itself. It becomes valuable when you use it to start conversations and ensure everybody has a shared understanding of what your product is and is not.

CREATE AN EXPERIMENT ROADMAP

An experiment roadmap is simply the prioritized list of assumptions (and their corresponding experiments) you plan to test with your target market to reduce the risk of building the wrong product. An experiment roadmap is not the same as a product roadmap. A product roadmap includes features that have been validated and you plan to include in your product. In contrast, an experiment roadmap consists of a list of assumptions and the experiments you'll use to test them. The outcome of those tests will eventually determine the product roadmap.

To create your experiment roadmap, work with your team to write down all the assumptions you've made so far. Your experiment roadmap can be as simple as a spreadsheet with these columns:

- Assumption

- Importance (low, medium, high)

- Amount of customer evidence (low, medium, high)

- Experiment to test the assumption

- Experiment success and fail criteria

Solution Planning

> **PRO TIP:** Some assumptions might benefit from more than one type of experiment. Therefore, your experiment roadmap can have multiple entries to address the same assumption.

To ensure you don't miss any potential risks to test, I recommend using your Solution Diagram to anchor the conversations with your team. Your Solution Diagram will provide context, helping you have richer conversations and avoid going into too many rabbit holes.

For each component in your Solution Diagram, facilitate a discussion with your team using open-ended questions, such as:

- What assumptions are we making around this component?

- What must be true for this assumption to be correct (or incorrect)?

- Which users will interact with this component?

- How much evidence do we have about the users involved with this component and about their pains?

- What unique capability could we provide to the user of this component that'd set our solution apart?

- What are some technical challenges we see when building or integrating this component?

- What assumptions are we making for this component, and how do we test those assumptions?

Answering these questions will give you all the information you need to create the first pass of your experiment roadmap.

Now that you have a list of assumptions, it's time to prioritize them. In their book, *Testing Business Ideas*, David Bland and Alexander Osterwalder introduce a helpful way to prioritize your assumptions. They recommend plotting your assumptions on a 2x2, where the Y-axis represents the importance of an assumption. The X-axis represents how much customer evidence you have around that assumption.

I like this approach because it helps your team visualize the items with the most significant risk, where you have little customer evidence. Those items should be prioritized at the top of your experimentation roadmap.

Solution Planning

> **PRO TIP:** Though I'll cover several types of experiments that work well in a B2B context, the book Testing Business Ideas is also a great resource if you are new to experimentation or would like a complete library of experiments.

GET STAKEHOLDER ALIGNMENT AND BUY-IN

It is essential to get alignment and buy-in from your leadership team at every stage of the innovation journey, but it is probably most important during this one. The Solution Planning stage is where the rubber meets the road. You are ready to present a vision of what a potential product could be and the steps on how you'll execute toward that vision. Your company needs to agree (or not) to go on this journey and invest in building a product based on the opportunity you identified.

I recommend meeting with your leadership team and Advisory Board to gain alignment on these six areas:

1. The solution you plan to build

2. The prioritized users you plan to pursue

3. Your experiment roadmap

4. Your approach to building and testing

5. Set expectation of uncertainty

6. The resources needed to move forward

Let me walk you through each area.

The Solution You Plan to Build

Leverage your Solution Diagram to illustrate your product's vision for your first ten customers and beyond. Emphasize that you'll start small, only focusing on the necessary components to support your prioritized users. Also, emphasize that you'll pursue an iterative, experimentation-driven approach. There's no guarantee that your final solution will be what you are showing in your Solution Diagram. Your product will change and adapt as you continue to gather and implement customer insights.

The Prioritized Users You Plan to Pursue

Emphasize that, as your product gains traction in the market, you can expand your solution to support other users and use cases. But at this point, the key is to start small to reduce waste and focus on the users that can give your product the potential to deliver value.

Your Experiment Roadmap

Share the evidence you have, the assumptions you are making, and the gaps you know you'll need to address. Show that you have a plan for gathering the information and letting them know how and how often you'll be sharing updates with new insights.

Your Approach to Building and Testing

This is probably the most important part and the one that is perhaps new to many people in your organization. Although you've performed a lot of customer discovery, you are still early in the process, so there is no certainty that your solution will meet the customer's needs. Therefore, to save time and avoid waste, you will not build the complete solution all at once using a Waterfall method. Instead, you'll focus on quick development iterations that help you test the market desirability, technical feasibility, and commercial viability of a potential product (i.e., Lean and Agile techniques). I describe how to accomplish this in the Prototyping stage, so make sure you read that chapter before going into this alignment meeting with your stakeholders.

Expectation of Uncertainty

When launching a new product to market, there is no certainty that you'll be successful. The process I outline in this book helps you reduce the risk of building something nobody wants, but there's no guarantee that you'll remove all risks or that you'll create a hit product. Your assumptions can be proven wrong, and you might need to go back to the drawing board. This means you might need to go back one or more stages of the journey. Make sure your leadership and Advisory Board understand this uncertainty and get buy-in into the process.

The Resources Needed to Move Forward

As you enter the Prototyping stage, you'll probably need access to additional resources. Since you'll be working in short iterations, you won't need a large development team yet, but you'll probably need a few more developers than what you have today. In addition, you might need support from people in other departments, such as legal or procurement. And you'll likely need help from business development and accounting as you get ready to close your first pilot customer.

REAL-WORLD STORY

Sasha led an innovation group inside a large organization that manufactured vending machines for consumer packaged goods (CPG) companies. The company's leadership team

Solution Planning

tasked Sasha to explore opportunities to add more value to their customers by incorporating some digital capabilities into their vending machines. Sasha's team talked to customers and prospects and learned that one of their biggest challenges was tracking inventory and product demand in the field. Once a vending machine was deployed in the field, the only way to know which products were selling and when the stock was running low was to send a person into the field to physically inspect the vending machine. This was inefficient, expensive, and prone to error.

Sasha's team saw an opportunity to create "smart vending machines" by adding sensors and intelligence to existing vending machines. The proposed solution would enable customers to track, in real-time, the inventory and sales generated by every smart vending machine around the world. Also, the system would allow their customers to monitor the health of each vending machine and automatically generate maintenance service requests if a vending machine was not working.

Sasha's leadership team loved the idea because it expanded their portfolio of products, and it solved a vital pain for their top customers. But although they were excited about the potential, they were not clear on what product they'd need to build to capture this market opportunity. Sasha's team had done a great job painting the big picture of how a fully operational solution would solve the customer's pain. Still, they hadn't taken the time to explain how her company would provide this solution. As a result, the executive team had questions and concerns about the feasibility and return on investment (ROI) of the solution.

They had questions like:

- What is the actual thing we are building?

- What does it mean to make our vending machines "smart"?

- Are we building new hardware and software?

- Will launching this product mean we are now in the inventory or sales tracking business?

- We are not in the maintenance business. How will that work?

To bring clarity, Sasha worked with her team to create a Solution Diagram that looked something like this:

Solution Planning

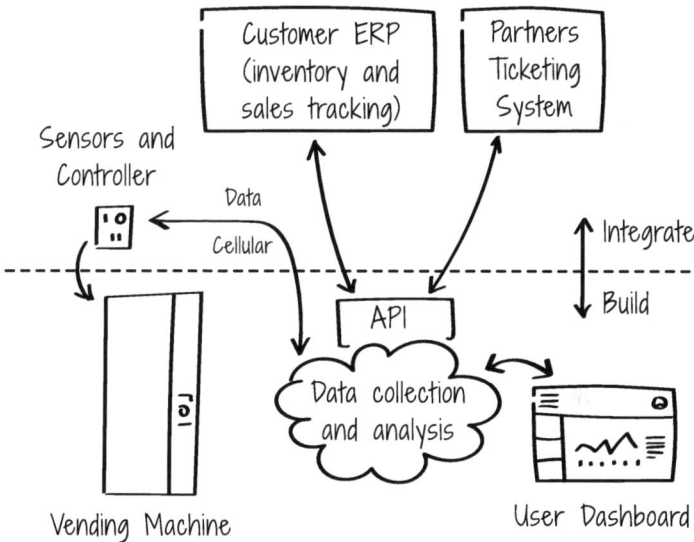

With the diagram, Sasha clarified the vision and brought alignment with her executive team and other departments involved in delivering the solution, including engineering and field operations. From the Solution Diagram, Sasha was able to clarify items like:

- To make our vending machines "smart," we'll need to add a few sensors and a controller with specialized software to track when a product is sold. We already identified companies that specialize in this technology, so we wouldn't reinvent the wheel. Instead, we will buy those items off-the-shelf and install them into our vending machines.

- From our customer's perspective, they'd buy the whole solution from us, but we'd only build the cloud software to aggregate, mine, and visualize the data coming from the vending machines.

- Our cloud software would expose APIs, enabling us to build connectors to the most common inventory and sales tracking systems. We are not in the business of replacing those systems. Instead, we need to connect with what the customer already has.

- We wouldn't go into the maintenance business either. Also, through APIs, we would integrate with our maintenance partners' systems. They would receive notifications when a machine needs service, and they'd handle it accordingly. This approach could open a new line of revenue because we can charge our partners to receive these maintenance notifications and charge our customers for the monitoring service.

The Solution Diagram helped Sasha convey the big picture of what the product could be in the future. But it also helped her explain that they wouldn't build all this functionality right away. Instead, they'd iterate building small portions of the solution and testing them with pilot customers. As a result, the Solution Diagram became an integral part of Sasha's roadmap, as it helped her explain which sections they were currently working on, which assumptions they were testing, and which features they'd be working on in the future.

Solution Planning

If you can prioritize users, create a Solution Diagram, create an experiment roadmap, and get alignment and support in the six areas I mentioned above, then congratulations! You are ready to move forward to the Prototyping stage.

But if you don't have full support or still have gaps in your planning, don't rush it. Take the time to plan and get that alignment. Your plan is very likely to change, so it's not about creating the perfect plan. Your goal is to think two or three steps ahead and ensure everybody is aligned to kickstart the next stage of the journey. Good luck!

Learn More

Here are some of my favorite books on sketching solutions, running experiments, and getting buy-in from your company on your proposed approach:

- *The Back of the Napkin: Solving Problems and Selling Ideas with Pictures* by Dan Roam

- *Pencil Me In: The Business Drawing Book for People Who Can't Draw* by Christina Wodtke

- *Value Proposition Design* by Alexander Osterwalder

- *Testing Business Ideas: A Field Guide for Rapid Experimentation* by David Bland and Alexander Osterwalder

Note: *For an extended list of books, the companion workbook, and additional resources, download your free B2B Innovator's Kit at https://danielelizalde.com/b2b-innovators-kit.*

Prototyping

I learned about the value of software Prototyping in a very roundabout way. Working at an industrial automation company, our customers would build prototypes all the time simply because their final product was too big and expensive to build without testing risky areas first.

I'm talking about some serious hardware and software prototypes here. For example:

- temperature chambers to test the performance of prototype car engines in extreme weather conditions;

- miniature cargo ship prototypes navigating a huge indoor pool to test if the ship would flip over during a storm, and

- prototypes of the Mars Rover landing gear to ensure it could land safely on Mars.

Although these prototypes were massive and very expensive, it was clear to me that building them was a lot faster, cheaper, safer, and less risky than building the real thing and testing it in the field.

But in the enterprise software world, I bumped into a very different paradigm. Many companies have a mentality that "it's just software," and therefore, it is easy to do. They should just build whatever they have in mind and fix it later, if needed (since it's just software). As you know by now, this approach is expensive and inefficient.

It wasn't until years later when I started working at a UX agency that I learned the techniques for creating rapid prototypes out of paper sketches and click-through documents. The techniques opened a world of opportunities for me. Just like the massive hardware prototypes I was familiar with, the simple sketches helped our customers reduce risk and test their ideas quickly for a fraction of the cost. Since then, I've been a huge advocate of those techniques.

As an Innovator, your goal is to reduce uncertainty and to bring products to market as fast as possible. To do that, you don't need to build the actual product to test most of your ideas. Believe me, you can validate many risky assumptions

Prototyping

with just a sketch or simple paper prototype. By doing this, you will accelerate your progress by months and months, for a fraction of the cost.

This chapter is all about testing your assumptions as fast as possible. I will share with you the tools and techniques I've learned throughout the years to minimize the amount of software you need to build to validate an idea. Once you embrace these tools, there is no going back. You'll be able to move at lightning speed, and you'll be on your way to delivering value to your customers and your company in record time.

The goal of the Prototyping stage is to present the simplest possible version of your proposed solution to your prospects and learn if it solves their pain. This means your goal is not to create a long roadmap of features and build your complete solution using a Waterfall approach. Not at all.

Your goal is to leverage the experiment roadmap you put together during the Solution Planning stage to build simple prototypes to test your assumptions. As you gain customer evidence that your prototype is going in the right direction, you'll evolve your prototype from simple sketches to clickable prototypes, to high-fidelity prototypes, and all the way to working prototypes your Champion is willing to pay for.

THE B2B INNOVATOR'S MAP

On the innovation journey, you are here:

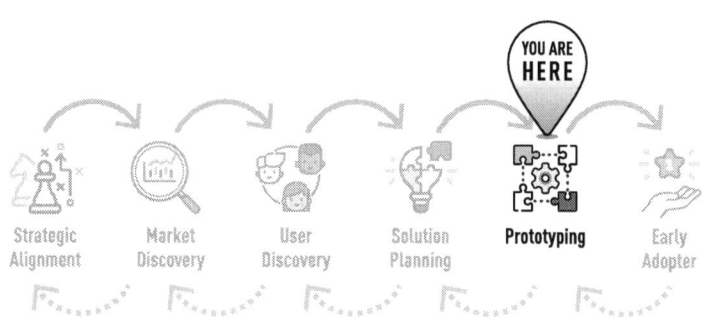

It is critical to understand that the innovation journey is not about building full-featured, robust solutions. Your goal is to find out if your proposed solution would solve your customer's pain while spending the least amount of time and money doing so. That's why I call this the Prototyping stage (and not the development stage). Keeping a Prototyping mindset will allow you to iterate, test fast, and discard anything that doesn't bring you closer to your first ten customers.

> **PRO TIP:** Avoid calling your prototype version 0.9, version 1, Alpha, MVP, or anything similar. To the rest of your company, such terms imply you have

Prototyping

> enough evidence to build the product and, therefore, you are in "build mode" as opposed to "innovation mode," making it harder to kill the initiative if you don't find market traction. I find it useful to give prototypes a code name, something catchy that people will remember, but it shows clearly that it's just a prototype that might never see the light of day. Code names can be names of places, animals, characters, or anything you can think of. For example, one of my favorite projects was "code name Pegasus." Coming up with that code name is always a fun exercise to do with your team.

The Prototype stage is all about increasing your chances of success by moving forward with evidence-based actions. To guide you through this stage of the B2B Innovator's Map, I've broken down this chapter into these four critical sections:

1. Resist the urge to build.

2. Test for desirability, feasibility, and viability.

3. Iterate towards your working prototype.

4. Get stakeholder alignment and buy-in.

Let me walk you through each of these areas.

RESIST THE URGE TO BUILD

The idea of creating simple prototypes to test assumptions and get market evidence might be new to your company, and therefore, you might get a lot of pushback. You'll probably hear objections like, "We need to build the product before getting any feedback" or "Customers won't talk to you unless you have a full product ready to sell" or "Showing prototypes will never work for our industry."

But that's simply not true. Some time ago, my team and I presented our proposed solution to our Champion, the Director of Operations at an electric utility. Our prototype was simply a series of sketches and fake screens built with sketching software. After our "demo," our Champion said, "This is exactly what we need. If you build that, I'll buy it from you." The Champion signed a letter of intent (LOI) and a few months later became our first customer. The moral of the story is that, if I was able to pull this off with a few sketches in a very traditional, highly-regulated industry, on a product that controls critical infrastructure, I'm sure the approach can work for you as well.

You've come a long way in reducing the risk of building a product nobody wants. Don't throw that away by giving in to the pressure of building an untested product concept. Hang in there!

TEST FOR DESIRABILITY, FEASIBILITY, AND VIABILITY

So what does it mean to test in a B2B context, and how do you do it? Since there are endless possibilities of things you can test, I find it helpful to organize testing into three categories:

1. **Market desirability:** Does your target market want the product you plan to build?

2. **Technical feasibility:** Can your company build, operate, and maintain this product?

3. **Commercial viability:** Can this product be profitable?

The desirability, feasibility, and viability framework has been around for some time and has become a common tool in many innovators' toolkits. Although it's hard to pinpoint who created this framework, many attribute it to the design consultancy IDEO, but they don't take the credit. I am grateful to whoever created it, and hopefully, in this book, I can contribute to its usefulness by applying it to B2B products.

There are no strict rules on how to test for desirability, feasibility, and viability. The only requirement is for your product to meet all three conditions. Your product must be desirable, feasible, *and* viable. If your product doesn't meet any one of those conditions, you should run more experiments or go back to previous stages of the B2B Innovator's Map to find a different approach.

> **PRO TIP:** It's up to you how long you should test before determining if your idea is not desirable, feasible, or viable. Just make sure to periodically take a step back and analyze if you could find traction with a few more tests or if you are just trying to run more experiments because you are afraid to recognize that your idea won't work.

Now that you are familiar with this simple framework, let's do a deep dive into the specific tools and techniques you can use to test your product's desirability, feasibility, and viability in a B2B context.

How to Test for Market Desirability

You've done a lot of work understanding your customer's pain and defining a potential solution. Unfortunately, many companies assume that their potential solution is the right solution, and that's why so many of them fail.

Desirability answers the question, "Does the market want my product?" Desirability is the most important attribute of any new product, and therefore, it's the area you should tackle first. If the market doesn't want your solution, it doesn't matter if your product is feasible or viable.

Testing desirability means getting customer evidence that your proposed solution solves your customer's pain in a better/faster/cheaper way than what they are currently doing. The only way to get that evidence is by engaging your prospects to get their feedback on your solution. You'll get the best feedback if you can put a solution in front of your customer and have them react to what you are proposing.

You should be able to convey the value proposition of your product with sketches, mockups, short videos, or simple prototypes. These prototypes are easy to build, and they are a very inexpensive way to test if your solution is going in the right direction.

Clickable Prototypes

The best way to get feedback on a product that doesn't yet exist is to build a clickable prototype. Your goal is to get customer feedback in rapid iterations, so don't waste time designing the look and feel of your prototype or simulating all the possible interactions a user could have with your product. Instead, focus on a series of rough sketches stitched together to simulate progressing through a workflow. Focus on a "happy path," if you will.

> **PRO TIP:** You don't need to build your prototype in code. Instead, you can create your clickable prototype using one of the many sketching and wireframing applications available in the market.

Here's an example of a clickable prototype:

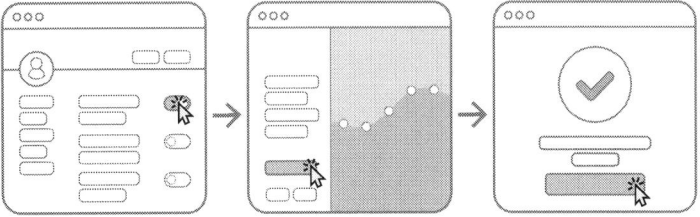

The goal of a clickable prototype is to facilitate conversations with your prospects. With every conversation, you'll gain more customer insights, and you'll continue to refine your prototype. Once you feel comfortable that your solution is going in the right direction, you can start working with your technical team to begin building a working prototype based on your findings. Keep in mind that even if you start building actual software, you can continue using clickable prototypes to get quick insights from your customers. Your goal is to iterate and get feedback as fast as possible, so don't let the software development process slow down your experiments.

Prototyping

When you are ready to start showcasing your clickable prototype, the best place to start is with all the people you already talked to during the Market and User Discovery stages. These are the people who already know you. You can test whether you understood their pains and verify that you have a solution for them.

Given all the different users involved in enterprise software, you'll need to divide your testing efforts between Champions and the User Ecosystem. For the personas you prioritized during the Solution Planning stage, your clickable prototype needs to showcase how your product can streamline their workflow and alleviate their pain. In contrast, since the Champion is responsible for the overall business outcome, they will be interested in a holistic solution to support their goals instead of a specific workflow for any individual user.

> **PRO TIP:** Build separate clickable prototypes for each of your personas. That will help you iterate quickly and focus on the area you are testing. Remember, you are not building your whole solution as one mammoth clickable prototype; you are just building the pieces that help you test your assumptions.

Testing for desirability is an iterative process, so it will take several iterations to fine-tune your clickable prototype. That's why it is important to iterate quickly by having simple prototypes you can adjust on the fly as you gain more customer insights. Aim for creating a new version of your prototype within a few hours instead of a few weeks or months. Moving at this speed takes planning, but it's worth the effort; by the time you start the actual building of your product, you'll have robust customer evidence that your solution is going in the right direction.

By the way, clickable prototypes are also helpful if you are building an API-based product targeted to developers. APIs can be challenging to understand for non-technical audiences, so I've found it beneficial to create mockups of applications that showcase what a user could build with your API or showcase the tools developers could use to build applications through your API. Overall, remember that a clickable prototype is just a tool to drive conversations and get feedback from your audience. As long as you can put something in front of them to react to, you'll be making progress towards gaining customer insights.

> **PRO TIP:** In addition to working closely with your prospects, make sure you present your clickable prototypes to your internal stakeholders as often as you can. These prototypes, along with your

> Solution Diagram, are great tools to keep your internal stakeholders up to date with your progress and for them to see how quickly you are incorporating customer feedback into a potential solution.

Experiments

When testing for desirability, your objective is to reduce the risk of launching a product nobody wants. Ideally, you'd showcase your prototype to 100 people or more to get as much evidence as possible. But given the complexities of accessing B2B prospects, that might not be doable. Therefore, you should consider other types of experiments that enable you to get as much information as possible, at scale and with the least amount of effort.

Your goal is to create easy-to-share assets and test them by putting them in front of as many people as possible. Example assets include a mockup brochure of your value proposition or a video with your value proposition and some animations showing a few workflows of your clickable prototype. These assets are easy to create and easy to update as you continue to gain new customer insights.

Once you have these assets, you need to decide how to make them available to your target audience to run the experiments. Some examples include:

- Creating a landing page on the web with your value proposition, your video, or your brochure.

- Becoming an exhibitor at an industry trade show (virtual or in-person).

- Organizing "lunch and learn" events with existing customers or prospects.

- Hosting a webinar and Q&A session focused on your customers' pains and presenting your solution (even if it's just a video or a clickable prototype).

These experiments must have a clear call to action so you can measure the interest of your target audience. People don't always do what they say. Therefore, actions provide more robust evidence than words.

For example, just monitoring the traffic on your landing page is not enough evidence of desirability. Instead, aim for engagement in one form or another, such as entering their email address to download the brochure, enrolling in a webinar to learn more, filling out a form asking for more information, or signing up for a demo (even if it's just of your early prototype). If people take these actions, you will have stronger evidence that they have the pain you discovered, and they are genuinely interested in your potential solution. Eventually, the strongest proof of desirability will come when customers offer to buy your product.

Prototyping

If your company is new to running experiments, they might get disillusioned after a few of the experiments fail. But the reality is that a large number of your experiments will fail, meaning that your assumptions were incorrect. That's great! It means you now have evidence of something that would not work, and you've saved your company a lot of time and money by not building a product based on false assumptions. Make sure you reiterate this philosophy to your team and your Advisory Board as frequently as possible. It's your role to keep them focused on the outcome and keep reinforcing that every failed experiment brings you a step closer in the right direction.

It is also essential to be realistic and set clear criteria for when to switch focus. After several failed experiments, it's a good idea to take a step back and evaluate if you should run more experiments or if you have enough evidence that your proposed solution is *not* desirable. Don't just keep running experiments, trying to find the one that will validate your assumptions. That's not the goal. If you have evidence that your solution might not be desirable, talk to your team and Advisory Board to agree on potential next steps. Your next move can include running more experiments or even going back to previous stages of the innovation journey to fine-tune your target market, User Ecosystem, or solution.

Running experiments takes planning, discipline, and practice, but they are well worth the effort. With some practice, you'll figure out which types of experiments work best for you, your company, and your industry. The critical thing to remember is that you need to run as many experiments as possible to improve your chance of success.

How to Test for Technical Feasibility

Once you have some evidence that your product is desirable, it's time to start looking at technical feasibility. Feasibility answers the question: "Can my company build, deploy, and operate this product?"

By working with dozens of teams, I've identified three types of feasibility areas you need to test for:

1. Development feasibility

2. Technology feasibility

3. Operational feasibility

Let's look at each one.

Development Feasibility

Development feasibility explores whether *your* company has the technical skills and resources to build the solution.

Prototyping

Notice I'm making a clear distinction between "Can *some* company build this product?" vs. "Can *your* company build this product?" This distinction is fundamental. I talk to many companies who misunderstand what it takes to build a complex SaaS or connected product and, therefore, underestimate the effort, skills, and risks involved. These companies fall into the trap of thinking that, if Google or Amazon can build this (or any) product, my company should be able to as well. But that's not a fair comparison. Unless you work for some technology powerhouse that has almost infinite resources and engineering prowess, then you need to be realistic and determine whether your team can pull it off.

Here are some examples that illustrate the importance of development feasibility:

- If your product relies on AI or machine learning, does your company have the data science team and skills required to pull off that work? And if you don't have those skills in-house, will your company be willing to invest in hiring or outsourcing these skills?

- Your company has traditionally built physical products, and you are new to digital technologies (e.g., cloud, APIs, AI). Will your company spin off a software team to build a solution and maintain it in the future? Do you have the engineering leadership to hire, train, and drive such a software team?

- Your company focuses on digital products, and your solution requires hardware. Will you be able to design and build the hardware in-house? Do you have the expertise and funding to outsource hardware development?

To test for development feasibility, I recommend discussing with your engineering leaders what it'd take to build the solution, including any significant risks they see. You can use your Solution Diagram to facilitate the feasibility discussion for each of the diagram components. Once you agree with engineering that, at a high level, your company is capable of delivering the solution, then the next step is to prioritize the most significant implementation risks, create hypotheses around those top risks, and run experiments to either validate or invalidate them.

> **PRO TIP:** If your company is not capable of building your solution today, but it still wants to pursue this opportunity, talk to your Advisory Board to discuss how to fill in that gap. Examples include hiring skilled people, outsourcing to a vendor, or collaborating with partners.

Technology Feasibility

Technology feasibility explores whether the technology your company plans to use is mature enough to support your solution.

If your company is building a solution with well-established technology, then the technology risk is much lower. For example, if you plan to deliver a SaaS solution based on a "standard" architecture (using a database, back-end services on the cloud, and an HTML-based user interface), your risk of technology feasibility is very low because these are mature technologies.

Now, I'm not implying that building solutions based on mature technology is easy. I'm just saying that the technology's risk of not supporting your solution is small. In other words, the risk of failure based on technology feasibility is minimal.

The risk of technology feasibility is higher when your solution leverages emerging technologies or technologies that are not mature enough to build and scale. For example, you might determine there's desirability and viability to deliver packages via autonomous drones. But is the technology ready to support this solution today?

To drive my point home, let me share a concrete example of technology feasibility. I worked with a team exploring a very innovative approach to cybersecurity on 5G cellular networks. We understood the customer's pain, and we had robust evidence of desirability. We also had a clear path to profitability since our viability experiments showed great promise. The most considerable risk was feasibility since, at the time, 5G technology was very new. After conducting several experiments, our engineering team concluded that our solution was not technically feasible. It wasn't for lack of technical skills, since we had top networking engineers on staff. Instead, the problem was that the 5G technology stack didn't enable the functionality required to support our application. In the future, that functionality might be available as part of the 5G standard, but until then, our proposed solution is unattainable. So we had to go back to the Solution Planning stage and come up with a different solution to tackle the customer pain we were after.

Here are a few insights I'd like to share from that experience:

- When working with cutting-edge technology, there is always the possibility that the technology is not mature enough for you to develop a complete solution.

- By taking the time to test our most significant technology risks, we determined early on that this idea was not technologically feasible, saving a lot of time and money.

- When working with cutting-edge technology, you'll find many unknowns because you are trailblazing new grounds. Therefore, you need to plan for the high likelihood that things won't work.

- When working with cutting-edge technology, sometimes the only way to know if something will work is to actually build it. Of course, I always advocate to test your ideas with low-effort experiments, but sometimes, you'll run into unknowns that will require your team to develop elaborate proofs of concept to find the answers.

Operational Feasibility

Assuming your team can build the solution (development feasibility) and that the technology supports your solution (technology feasibility), the last area to test for is operational feasibility. Operational feasibility asks the question, "Can we deploy, operate, and maintain this solution?"

Your product will fail the operational feasibility tests if the requirements to deploy and operate your solution fall outside of what your company is willing or able to do.

Here are a few situations that might cause your solution to fail the operational feasibility tests:

- Your proposed solution falls outside your company's strategy, and your leadership team is not open to considering this new approach. For example, your customer requires you to provide a service in conjunction with your product. However, your company strategy focuses on being a "product" company and is unwilling to provide professional services.

- Your solution has a dependency you can't overcome, such as not having access to data.

- Your solution has an operational requirement that makes it impossible for your company to support. For example, you need to install at remote locations or secure areas where you are not likely to get access.

- There is a regulation that makes it impossible for you to proceed. This is common with solutions in highly regulated markets, such as energy and healthcare. Another example is drones, which in the US are regulated by the Federal Aviation Administration (FAA), which is the arbiter of where drones can fly and for what purpose.

- Your business model is based on leveraging the scale of the public cloud, but your customer wants to run your solution on-premise or on their private cloud.

You can get a good idea of the operational requirements for your solution by talking to your Champions, the User Ecosystem, and industry experts inside or outside your company. Unfortunately, you won't know the full scope of the operational challenges until you deploy your first solution. You'll learn a lot more about that in the Early Adopter stage as you start working with your first ten customers. But, for now, it's a good idea to have this conversation with your prospects and your teams and be aware of any potential red flags that might lie ahead.

How to Test for Commercial Viability

Viability answers the question, "Can this product generate a significant financial return for my company?"

Testing viability is critical because you need some level of assurance that the investment your company is about to make (or is already making) has a path to profitability. Otherwise, the impact on your company is two-fold. First, you don't make any money, but second, you incur an opportunity cost. If you spend too much time chasing something that is not financially viable, then you are not pursuing some other initiatives that might be. Explaining to your leadership team why your team spent so much time and money on a venture that had no chance of returning a profit is a terrible place to be. Believe me, I know.

Testing viability involves running experiments to gain evidence on whether your customer's pain is big enough

that they are willing to buy your product at a price that generates a profit.

Notice that testing viability involves engaging your prospects to get factual market evidence instead of just imagining some profit calculations on a spreadsheet. I can't tell you how many business plans and spreadsheets I've seen that show rapid market adoption, tremendous growth, and big profits. Everything is nicely plotted quarterly with a line trending up. Now, don't get me wrong, I'm not saying you shouldn't work with your finance and business teams to create these financial scenarios. But my point is that these calculations should only be directional and must be tested. For example, your spreadsheet calculations might have different growth curves based on various price points or contract durations, and you won't know which one (if any) will resonate in the market. These various growth curves should become hypotheses for you to test with real customers.

The good news is that by complementing traditional business model calculations with an experimentation mindset, you get the best of both worlds. You are leveraging the expertise of other departments to inform your hypotheses, and you are running experiments to gather evidence on whether those models can be profitable.

Throughout the years, I've discovered four types of viability testing you should focus on:

1. Viability of your value proposition

2. Viability based on switching costs

3. Viability based on special component/service costs

4. Internal viability

Let's explore these types of commercial viability.

Viability of Your Value Proposition

When testing for the viability of your value proposition, you are looking for evidence that your customer is willing to pay for your particular solution and that the amount they are willing to pay meets your financial projections.

There are many experiments you can run to test the viability of your value proposition. When you are just getting started, the best approach is to go back to the Champion you've talked to before and interview them to learn how much they'd be willing to pay for your solution. These interviews will give you an idea of a monetary figure, but most importantly, they'll help you understand why they believe your solution is worth that much. It could be due to budgetary constraints, purchasing cycles, existing solutions in the market, etc. Your job is to discover as much information as you can.

It might be hard for your Champions to share how much they are willing to pay. Instead, you can use the information you gathered in the Market Discovery stage to quantify their pain. A rule of thumb is that you can price your solution at 10-15 percent of the amount of your customer's pain. For example, if your customer is losing $10M per year due to this pain, they might be willing to pay you $1M to solve this pain. This is not set in stone, but it gives you a good place to start your conversations.

Conversations with your Champions will give you good insights, but I would not consider them strong evidence yet. There's always a big gap between what a prospect says and what they will do. In contrast, strong evidence of viability happens when a prospect is ready to buy your solution.

Here are additional viability experiments that encourage action and gauge your prospect's intent to buy:

- Create a mock brochure with your value proposition, features, and pricing. Then, discuss the brochure with prospects and get their reaction to your proposed price vs. value.

- Run a webinar describing your solution and pricing. The webinar's call-to-action can be to enroll in your upcoming (paid) beta program. Even if you don't have a beta program yet, you can still test viability by having people register. Remember, you are looking for the intent to buy.

- Become an exhibitor at a trade show to demo your product (even if you only have a clickable prototype). Ask people to sign up for your beta program.

- Create a sales pitch deck and present it to prospects. Ask interested people to give you a letter of intent (LOI) or a small deposit to signal their commitment to purchase the solution when the first version is ready.

When designing these experiments, it is critical to test your solution's pricing, packaging, and monetization model. That way, you'll get a better understanding of which combinations are more likely to make your product viable. For example, your customer might like your solution and agree with the price, but you need to package a different set of features in your offering to convince them. Or maybe the issue is not price but your monetization model. For example, you might be offering your product as a one-time sale, but your customers would be more comfortable with a subscription model. Testing multiple angles is important, especially when you've found desirability but you struggle to find evidence of viability.

Viability Based on Switching Costs

From your customer's perspective, the cost of a new enterprise solution is much more than the price of the product itself. Customers look at your product from a total cost of ownership perspective and determine if the value they'll get once the solution is deployed is worth the time and money to get there. This includes the time and cost associated with:

- Installing and configuring a new enterprise solution.

- Migrating data from existing systems to the new solution.

- Integrating the new solution with existing corporate systems.

- Training the User Ecosystem to be efficient with the new solution.

- Training IT or partners to support and maintain the new solution.

Once a customer purchases an enterprise product, it becomes "sticky," meaning that the effort and cost of switching to a new solution become prohibitive unless the value is exponentially greater than what they are getting today.

I'm sure you've seen many companies operating with outdated systems, such as payroll or expense tracking, just because the pain and cost of switching to a better solution are so significant that it eclipses the potential benefits of a new solution.

Prototyping

That is excellent news if your solution is the one that's already sticky. But it's terrible news if you are trying to displace an existing solution.

Understanding how burdensome switching costs are for your target audience is vital. For example, you might find that your target audience is eager to move on from their current systems, and switching costs are not an issue. In contrast, you might find that the pain of switching to your new solution is so enormous that you are not likely to get any customers to switch.

> **PRO TIP:** Listen for opportunities to mitigate switching costs, such as providing automated migration tools or offering integration and training for free. These opportunities could enhance your offering and remove friction, enabling you to get your foot in the door.

If you conclude that your product is not viable due to switching costs, talk to your Advisory Board and consider going back to the Market Discovery stage to select a different target market. Look for a market where the incumbent solution is less ingrained into your prospect's enterprise, and they are, therefore, more willing to try out a new solution.

Viability Based on Special Component/Service Costs

This section doesn't apply to every product, but it's worth discussing it with your team just to eliminate another potential risk: when one or more of the components of your solution is very expensive, you can price yourself out of the market (or out of profitability) because the price of your overall solution is beyond your customer's willingness to pay.

This situation is common if your solution includes hardware components, complex integrations, or expensive installations. For example, I used to work at a company developing AI-powered energy storage solutions for commercial buildings. At the time, the cost of batteries was very high, so the cost/value relationship was not very attractive for our customers. In our case, we were able to leverage renewable energy incentives from the government and other financial vehicles, which made the overall cost of our software + hardware solution more palatable. In addition, we benefited from the ever-improving cost-curves of batteries, where every year, batteries kept getting cheaper, making our solution more attractive.

If your product includes hardware, custom components, or specialized services, you might find yourself in this situation. I recommend revisiting your Solution Diagram with your team to identify any unique components that can affect the overall viability of your solution and discuss potential ways to get around them. Keep in mind that you don't need to solve the cost or profit challenge for your first ten customers since, at that point, you are still in learning mode, and your goal is not to deliver a profit yet. But this analysis is essential because if you don't see a path to profitability in the future due to unique components or services, you might need to go back to the Solution Planning stage and come up with a different approach.

Internal Viability

Viability is not only a measure of the market's willingness to pay. It is also a measure of your company's desire to invest in building, operating, and maintaining a new product. I call this willingness to invest "internal viability."

Testing for internal viability might seem counterintuitive. After all, if your company already approved exploring this opportunity, why wouldn't they support the product that results from that exploration?

The reason is that innovation, by definition, is full of uncertainty. You will encounter uncertainty around the market's needs and uncertainty around the solution your team could create to meet those needs. In other words, your company has only approved the opportunity for exploration. They haven't approved the development of a new product because, until this stage, nobody knew what such a product could be. Once your company understands the opportunity and the solution you propose to build to capitalize on that opportunity, your company might decide they are unwilling to invest in that particular solution. That's why it's important to test for internal viability early and often.

Here are a few reasons why your proposed solution might not be well received by your company:

- You found an opportunity in an adjacent market, and your company is not ready to move in that direction.

- You are proposing a different business model from what your company uses today (i.e., subscriptions vs. transactional sales), and your company is not willing or able to adopt that new model.

- Your company is willing to try a new business model, but they can't operate in that model. For example, you are proposing a subscription model, and your company doesn't have the legal, accounting, or automation infrastructure to run a subscription business.

- Your product will require specialized sales, marketing, and operations support because it targets a persona or market you are not servicing today.

- There is no additional capacity in the engineering teams to take on this new product. You'd need to hire a whole new team or drop something from another product's roadmap, and your company might not be open to that.

- If you work at an established company, the "innovation antibodies" might kick in. Although other business units said they'd support the direction of your new product, now that the prospect of a new product is here, business-as-usual takes over. Leaders in the organization are not willing to divert resources into this new initiative. Either they don't have any resources to spare (which is often the case), or they fear that this initiative might eat into their existing business.

The key to testing internal viability is constant communication with your Advisory Board and leaders across the organization. Share your findings and direction often so that you can constantly gauge if they are comfortable with the direction of your innovation journey. Above all, avoid surprises. You don't want to go too deep into testing or development without ensuring that your company will back you up.

A FEW RECOMMENDATIONS

The Prototyping stage spans from testing your initial sketches with customers all the way to iteratively developing your product until you have a working prototype that a prospect could potentially buy. This part of the process requires constant iteration between testing and development to ensure you are building the right product that solves the pain of your Champion and User Ecosystem.

I covered a lot of ground in this chapter, so before moving on to the last stage in the B2B Innovator's Map, I'd like to share a few lessons I've learned the hard way.

Test Desirability First

I can't emphasize this enough. Having a feasible and viable product means nothing if customers don't want it. Before investing in product development, make sure you have strong customer evidence that your target market desires your product.

Finding desirability won't happen on your first try, so don't be discouraged. If you understand your customer's pain, then continue iterating with your team until you find a solution that meets your customers' needs and that they are willing to pay for. Keep trying. You'll get there!

Involve a Multi-Disciplinary Team

By involving product, design, engineering, and business teams in the experimentation and Prototyping process, you'll move faster and get automatic buy-in from other departments, not only on the process but also on the outcomes. On the other hand, if you don't involve different teams, you'll miss out on their valuable input, and then you'll have to do additional work to get their buy-in further down the road.

Iterate Quickly and As Much As Possible

Your goal is to test your assumptions as quickly as possible so that you can reduce risk and continue building based on customer evidence. Aim for short, two-to-four-week iterations. Know that running some of these experiments in the B2B world will probably take longer, and that's OK. I'm not saying you'll be able to run 100 experiments in a week, as you would in B2C, but I'm saying you should iterate as fast as possible within the constraints of your company and your industry.

Define Clear Criteria for Validating Each Assumption

Make sure you clearly define the criteria for validating or invalidating every assumption in your experiment roadmap. Unfortunately, many companies new to experimentation miss this part. The result is innovation theater because the projects linger forever as zombie products, or the teams just build whatever they planned to make anyway. Testing becomes just a checkbox to say they did it instead of a critical tool to help them reduce risk.

Iterate Towards Your Working Prototype

Earlier in this chapter, I mentioned you must resist the urge to build early on. When you start the Prototyping stage, focus on learning and testing all of your assumptions around desirability, feasibility, and viability. But once you have enough customer evidence that you are going in the right direction, then it's OK to start building.

But remember, you are not building a full-featured product in a Waterfall way. What I mean is that you should build your product iteratively, focusing on the core architecture and the user flows where you have the most evidence.

I recommend building your software in small, iterative chunks, ensuring that every feature you are developing is desirable, feasible, and viable. Your goal is to build just enough functionality to entice a Champion to become your first customer.

This is the time to leverage concepts like Agile and Lean. If you are new to Agile and Lean, refer to the Learn More section at the end of this chapter for more information.

GET STAKEHOLDER ALIGNMENT AND BUY-IN

As you transition to the Early Adopter stage, it's a good idea to get together with your Advisory Board and leadership team to get alignment and continued buy-in. Here are four critical areas of alignment you need:

1. Agreement that testing and building is an ongoing process

2. Agreement that the focus is still on learning, not revenue

3. Agreement that your company is ready to manage your first sale

4. Agreement on the additional people needed to move forward

Let's look at each item in more detail.

Agreement That Testing and Building Is an Ongoing Process

Testing and building based on customer insights does not stop in the Prototyping stage. Your team needs to continue this iterative practice during the Early Adopter stage and beyond. **The only difference between stage five and stage six will be what you test, how you test it, and what you build.**

Most companies believe that understanding your customers is either not necessary or that it's just an upfront, one-time activity. That's why so many companies stop the learning process once they get an inkling of evidence and focus only on development. Unfortunately, as I've said multiple times, that approach leads to waste and ultimately to products nobody wants to buy.

You must get buy-in from your leadership team to continue working in small, iterative chunks that alternate between discovery and delivery.

Agreement That the Focus Is Still on Learning, Not Revenue

Having a customer willing to pay for your working prototype will trigger numerous emotions inside your company. Many people will be excited, happy, and even relieved. At this point, it is not uncommon for your stakeholders to start thinking about your product as a new source of revenue for the company. But although that's the ultimate goal, you are not there yet. The Early Adopter stage is still focused on learning and ensuring you can deliver value to your first ten customers.

Your leadership team must understand and agree that the revenue you'll get from the first ten customers is just an indication that you are going in the right direction. **In other words, you need to make it clear that the goal of working with your first ten customers is to learn and not to make a profit.**

The key is to remember that your customer is buying a working prototype, and they know you are early in the development process. Your customer is taking a risk by trying out your new solution, and they know you'll require a good amount of their time as you fine-tune your offering.

Prototyping

At this stage, you are not sure you'll be able to deliver on the value you promised (that's what the Early Adopter stage is for). Therefore, your first ten customers might pay a significantly reduced fee for your product, or the payment terms might be deferred until you deliver value. In short, your company needs to adopt a learning mindset and not count on this revenue to meet any short-term financial goals.

Agreement That Your Company Is Ready to Manage Your First Sale

As part of your internal viability tests, make sure that your company is ready to sell your working prototype when the time comes. This might sound obvious, but you'd be surprised at how many companies get to this point and don't have a clear plan on how to close those initial sales.

To avoid this issue, bring up this topic with your Advisory Board early on. Work with your various stakeholders on a plan that includes:

- The necessary legal agreements to sell a new product (e.g., contracts, letter of intent, terms and conditions, liability, ownership of intellectual property, payment terms, service level agreements).

- A process to collect and recognize revenue coming from your innovation initiative. If you are a startup and this is your first sale, you might not have the processes and systems to invoice and collect money from customers. And if you are part of an established company, you might need to circumvent your standard new product introduction (NPI) process, including creating new SKUs, price lists, sales enablement, etc. None of that applies to your product this early in the journey.

Agreement on the Additional People Needed to Move Forward

In the Early Adopter stage, you'll run quick iterations to learn and deliver value to your first customer. And in addition to making this one customer successful, you also need to focus on testing and implementing new functionality that will help you close your second, third, and tenth customers.

Before entering the Early Adopter stage, make sure you work with your team to define the additional resources you'll need in this new stage. You will probably need additional designers and engineers to continue testing and building, as well as support from sales or business development to actively pursue customers two through ten.

Getting support from business development is vital because the product team will be jam-packed delivering value for the first customer, so they won't have the bandwidth to drive the funnel to close customers two through ten. A common practice is to create a small business development team, often called a "tiger" or "delta" team. Their goal is to mine existing customers interested in the new product or going out to the market to close new sales. The work of the tiger team is critical not only for closing additional early customers, but also for gaining feedback from the market on your product's positioning, value proposition, sales pitch, and even for continuing to test pricing packages.

REAL-WORLD STORY

Testing for desirability, feasibility, and viability and incorporating your findings into the development process can be messy. The evidence you find along the way might not be conclusive, and at times it might seem contradictory. This is normal, and it's all part of the process. I want to share a real-world example to illustrate this complexity.

Fernando worked at a company that built the hardware and software for autonomous guided vehicles (AGVs) used for manufacturing. Think of these AGVs as small trays with wheels that autonomously navigate a manufacturing plant carrying raw materials, components, or a finished product from one place to another. Fernando's team was tasked with exploring opportunities to improve their customers' operational efficiency.

After talking to many plant managers (the Champion), Fernando discovered that a common pain was when the AGVs stalled in areas where the Wi-Fi signal was weak. A stalled AGV caused delays in the production line and required somebody from the factory's staff to manually pick up the AGV and carry it to an area with better connectivity. This resulted in lost efficiency, which impacted the manufacturing facility's bottom line.

Fernando's team saw an opportunity to deliver a next-generation AGV powered by new connectivity technologies. They quickly decided to try cellular connectivity, specifically 5G, since this new technology promised to fix many of the "blind spots" inherent to Wi-Fi. However, before jumping into a significant development effort, Fernando wanted to test the riskiest hypotheses, including:

- **Desirability:** Will customers purchase 5G-powered AGVs if we promise to solve the stalling problem?

- **Feasibility:** Can we develop, deploy, and operate 5G-powered AGVs?

- **Viability:** Is solving the stalling issue valuable enough for customers to pay a premium for 5G-powered AGVs? Are the switching costs of moving from Wi-Fi to 5G acceptable for our customers?

Fernando's team conducted a few experiments to test their hypotheses. After a few weeks of testing, the results

Prototyping

were promising. First, they discovered that an AGV with no connectivity blind spots is a desirable solution, and in fact, several people they talked to were interested in buying one right away. Then, to test technical feasibility, the team put together a proof of concept to understand the nuances of operating AGVs with 5G. The results were also promising since they were able to operate their prototype in a 5G network, and they demonstrated that they could solve the stalling issues. But this is where they started to run into problems.

Since 5G was a new technology, it was difficult and expensive to source the parts they needed. That meant the final design would be significantly more costly than their current Wi-Fi version. They also ran into issues when testing for operational feasibility. They discovered that to operate 5G indoors, they would need to deploy a private 5G network dedicated to that building. This would result in additional cost and deployment time, plus it would make this solution not viable based on switching costs alone (from Wi-Fi to 5G). Another issue around switching costs came to light when Fernando's team interviewed the User Ecosystem. They discovered that the IT team was not excited about that solution because everything else in the factory runs on Wi-Fi. The IT staff didn't know how to operate, troubleshoot, or maintain a cellular network, so they were concerned about their ability to support this initiative. Last but not least, Fernando's team discovered that cellular networks required a licensed spectrum, meaning you need to pay a telecommunications carrier a monthly premium just to operate the network. This would add another layer of cost and complexity to the solution since they'd need to involve a telecom carrier in each deployment.

Although the customer was excited (and willing to pay) for solving the blind-spot problem, the solution proposed by Fernando's team was not the right one. It was desirable and feasible, but it wasn't viable in terms of price, switching costs, and special components (availability of 5G radios). The good news was that, by conducting these experiments, Fernando's team was able to quickly reject the 5G-powered solution before investing many months and millions of dollars developing a product that customers would not buy.

Another positive outcome of quickly iterating between testing and building their idea was that, although the 5G solution didn't work out, they discovered that the need to solve the "blind spot" issue was a real opportunity. Therefore, Fernando and his team went back to the drawing board to explore other potential solutions to solve this problem (i.e., they went back to the Solution Planning stage). With all the customer insights they now had, they came up with a new potential solution based on Wi-Fi 6. This new solution had most of the benefits of the 5G version, but it didn't require deploying a private cellular network. And it didn't have any significant switching costs since Wi-Fi 6 is very similar to the version of Wi-Fi the IT teams were already familiar with. Fernando's team ran a similar set of experiments for Wi-Fi 6-powered AGVs and quickly found customer evidence for

Prototyping

desirability, feasibility, and viability. So they moved forward, creating their working prototype, and quickly closed their first ten customers.

As you make progress testing your assumptions and building a solution based on customer evidence, you'll get to a point where you'll have a working prototype your prospects want to buy. If you find yourself in this position, congratulations!

Getting your first customer is the gate for advancing into the Early Adopter stage. You've found the ultimate validation for desirability, feasibility, and viability. Most products never get their first paying customer, so feel proud that you've made it farther than most companies out there.

Learn More

Here are a few helpful books I recommend to supplement your knowledge:

- *Testing Business Ideas: A Field Guide for Rapid Experimentation* by David Bland and Alexander Osterwalder

- *Sprint: How to Solve Big Problems and Test New Ideas in Just Five Days* by Jake Knapp

- *Running Lean: Iterate from Plan A to a Plan That Works* by Ash Maurya

- *Agile Product Management with Scrum* by Roman Pichler

Note: Get an extended list of books, the companion workbook, and additional resources by downloading your B2B Innovator's Kit at https://danielelizalde.com/b2b-innovators-kit.

Early Adopter

PILOT PROJECTS OFFER A UNIQUE OPPORTUNITY TO LEARN and make progress toward your first ten customers. But if not managed correctly, they can go terribly wrong, causing you to damage the relationship with potential customers and even derailing your overall innovation initiative.

Laura was responsible for a new line of manufacturing automation solutions. Her team had completed the previous five stages of the innovation journey and was ready to deploy their working prototype to her first potential customers. To her surprise, her first customer was one of the biggest contract manufacturing companies in the world.

The first red flag was that the customer didn't want to pay anything for the pilot project. They used their company's size and reputation as a big carrot for Laura's team. If the pilot were successful, they said, they'd roll out Laura's new product around the world. Laura's leadership team saw a big opportunity and decided to ignore the red flags and fund the pilot project anyway. But the issues continued. The customer was very slow to provide feedback or engage with the solution, causing months of delays. And with every interaction, they kept changing the scope of the pilot project by adding new feature requests, additional integrations with corporate systems, and so on. There was no end in sight.

You can probably see where this story is going. After many months of hard work, the customer informed Laura they'd decided to purchase an off-the-shelf solution from a major automation player. Just like that, the pilot project was over, and Laura's company had nothing to show for it.

There were many warning signs along Laura's journey, but most of them were ignored because Laura and her leadership team had misaligned expectations. Instead of treating this pilot project as one of ten initial customers to learn from, Laura's company was star-struck by the brand and potential of this one customer. They latched on to short-term profit instead of learnings that would unleash sustainable gains in the mid-term.

As a result, Laura's company shut down this emerging product line since they couldn't afford to lose any more money on it. This decision had a double impact. Not only did they lose a lot of money on the pilot, but by terminating the initiative, they abandoned the opportunity to create a new product line that was desirable in the market and could have generated significant new revenues for the company.

Early Adopter

In this story, Laura's company ignored many warning signs along the way. But the two biggest ones include 1) thinking of this initial customer as a source of revenue instead of a source of learning, and 2) failing to recognize they were working with a pragmatist instead of an early adopter.

In this chapter, I break down these and many other early signs of trouble so you can identify them quickly and work with your team to avoid catastrophic pilot projects. Pilot projects give you an amazing opportunity to learn. If you keep an eye out for the challenges I describe in this chapter, you'll be on your way to delivering value to your first ten customers!

In his book, *Crossing the Chasm*, Geoffrey Moore defines early adopters as the people within a company who have intense pain and are willing to try new solutions, even if these solutions haven't been proven on the market yet. **I named this stage the Early Adopter stage because your first ten customers must be early adopters. Your goal is to deliver value to these ten customers via your unproven solution.**

As you might recall from Chapter 1, you want to work with ten pilot customers before making any next-step decisions because you want to minimize the risk of variability between multiple enterprise customers. I know it is tempting to start thinking about scale after just a couple of successful pilot projects but hang in there. Most of the things that can go wrong with new deployments will happen within your first ten pilot customers.

THE B2B INNOVATOR'S MAP

According to the B2B Innovator's Map, you are here:

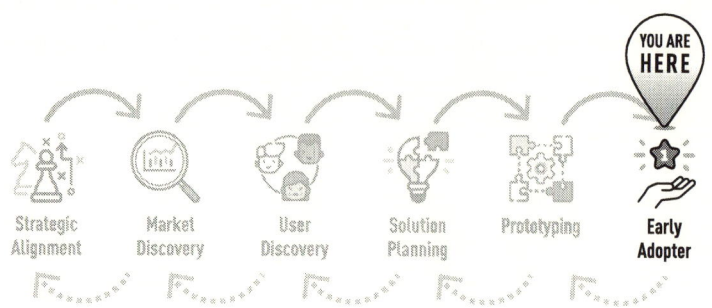

As you work with your first, second, and tenth customers, you will learn what it takes for your product to deliver value. Since most new products die during the pilot stage, this chapter focuses on best practices you can use to increase your chances of success while running pilot programs with your first ten customers.

These best practices include:

- Seven principles of successful pilot programs

- Four techniques to move fast, build less, and learn more

- Eight areas where you should not cut corners

But before getting into the best practices for running successful pilot programs, let's take a step back and discuss why B2B customers have pilot programs in the first place.

WHY B2B CUSTOMERS REQUIRE PILOT PROGRAMS

You are hopeful that your solution will help your Champion achieve their goal. But at this point, neither you nor your customer is 100 percent certain your untested solution can deliver on that value.

Put yourself in your Champion's shoes. From their perspective, there is a significant risk in testing your solution. If your product doesn't deliver on its promise, then your Champion takes multiple hits. First, she will have wasted the money invested in your product. Second, she will have lost time in making progress towards her goal. And third, she will take a hit on her reputation since she selected a product that didn't work. Given what's at stake, it is not surprising that pilot programs are standard practice in enterprise software. A pilot allows the Champion to start small by testing a new solution in a contained environment, such as a testbed or sandbox.

The type of contained environment depends on the type of product and industry you are selling into. For example:

- If you sell software for the manufacturing sector, a pilot can run on a single manufacturing line in one of your customer's manufacturing facilities.

- If you sell CRM software, a pilot could involve testing your software with a small portion of your customer's sales team.

- If you sell eCommerce software, a pilot might include only a small part of the customer's catalog.

- If you sell energy efficiency solutions for retailers, a pilot might be confined to a single retail store.

Unfortunately, running successful pilot programs is very difficult. Most B2B products never make it beyond the pilot stage, and as a result, these products are not rolled out to the rest of the customer's organization. The most frequent reason why pilot programs fail is that the product could not solve the customer's pain. And in most cases, it is because the vendor didn't clearly understand that pain. Based on all the work you've done throughout the previous five stages of the innovation journey, I don't believe you will have that problem. But to increase your chance of success, let's look at seven principles that will help you navigate the complexity of pilot programs.

SEVEN PRINCIPLES OF SUCCESSFUL PILOT PROGRAMS

The more you know about the challenges ahead, the better prepared you will be to address them. Here are my seven principles to increase your chances of success when running a pilot program:

1. Work with early adopters.

2. Define clear success criteria.

3. Define a manageable scope for your pilot.

4. Deliver value for the Champion first and the User Ecosystem second.

5. Plan for unengaged customers.

6. Be ultra-responsive.

7. Avoid items that can delay (and derail) your pilot.

Let's look at each principle in more detail.

Work with Early Adopters

Since your product hasn't been established in the market, each of the Champions of your first ten customers must be early adopters. They must be willing to try your untested solution, *and* they must be open to partnering with you to co-create version one of your product.

In contrast to early adopters, Geoffrey Moore defines the people with little tolerance for risk as *pragmatists*. They mitigate risk by only buying products already proven in the market and adopted by similar companies. Pragmatists expect a full-featured product, ready to be rolled out at scale. During the Early Adopter stage, a common mistake is to start working with pragmatists instead of early adopters. **Working with**

pragmatists this early in the game creates a mismatch of expectations between what you can provide and what a pragmatist expects. This mismatch is a significant cause of pilot failure.

Targeting pragmatists with new products is most common in established companies with successful products already on the market. This is because they want to offer their latest solutions to existing customers (usually pragmatists).

A common misconception is that startups are early adopters and large companies are pragmatists. That is not the case. As Geoffrey Moore clarified during our podcast interview, the terms early adopter and pragmatist refer to people within a company and not the company itself. There are early adopters within large companies and pragmatists within startups.[2] Your task is to identify who is who and work with early adopter Champions instead of pragmatist Champions who only want to purchase mature products for immediate rollout.

Define Clear Success Criteria

The goal of the Early Adopter stage is to deliver value to your first ten customers so you can move on to larger pilots and eventually to company-wide deployments. But you can't get there if you don't have an explicit agreement with your Champion

---

2   https://danielelizalde.com/geoffrey-moore/

as to what value means, how to measure it, and how to know when you get there. Many pilot projects die just because there isn't a clear understanding of what success looks like. Having these discussions early on is crucial to your success.

Defining success criteria with your customer involves agreeing on a clear outcome you need to achieve and a metric you can demonstrate as a measure of success. These metrics are easier to define if your product helps with automated processes. You could agree that your solution will improve automated test times on the manufacturing floor by 10 percent or that you will reduce their energy bill by 20 percent.

Defining similar metrics for manual processes is much harder because your system doesn't have full control of your customer's process. For example, if your solution claims that it can help the sales team convert 15 percent more leads, then it'll be hard to demonstrate success because you are at the expense of many factors, including the performance of the individual members of the sales team. For these situations, you need to get creative and work with your Champion to define some metrics you can measure (and control), as well as agree to get qualitative feedback from your User Ecosystem describing how your solution is better than the alternative.

In many cases, defining the success criteria comes down to trust and the strength of the relationship you have with your Champion. Always aim for measurable goals, but realize that sometimes it's just not possible to get them.

Define a Manageable Scope for Your Pilot

As the scope of your pilot grows, so does the risk of delivering on your value proposition. Examples of large scope include:

- Deploying to a large number of sites

- Supporting a large number of users

- Requiring deep integrations with existing corporate systems

- Developing too many custom features

If you find yourself in this situation, talk to your Champion to understand their intent. **The pilot's goal should be to demonstrate key characteristics of your new product, not to mimic a full enterprise deployment at a smaller scale.** A Champion asking for an enormous pilot scope (even if they are willing to pay for it) should raise red flags for your team. It could mean that you are dealing with a pragmatist who needs to deploy a full-featured solution just to evaluate your product.

As a side note, notice I mentioned "developing too many custom features." Co-creating a new product with early adopters will always result in creating features aimed at that particular customer's needs. You need to balance making this customer successful and becoming a custom development shop for this customer. Since you understand the pains of your target market, make sure you always evaluate your Champion's request against your overall product vision.

The rule of thumb is only to build features that will benefit multiple customers; otherwise, your product will become a one-off solution. If you are not sure about the value of a particular feature, talk to your engineering team to determine how to build the feature with minimal effort or in a way that makes it easy to decouple from the main product (via APIs). That's why it's critical to work with ten pilot customers, so you have a way to compare and contrast what is essential for a single customer vs. the majority of your target market.

Deliver Value for the Champion First and the User Ecosystem Second

The only way to deliver value to your early customers is by convincing the Champion that your product can help them achieve their business outcome. But this outcome can only be achieved through the combined output of the people in your User Ecosystem. Therefore, your pilot program needs to include all the necessary, functional features to empower critical personas in your User Ecosystem to complete their core workflows.

But during the Early Adopter stage, your goal is to deliver value towards the Champion's desired business outcome, even if that means sacrificing some of the experience for the rest of your User Ecosystem.

For example, if you are building an enterprise recruiting system and the key outcome you need to demonstrate is your ability to suggest the best candidates based on your selection criteria, your pilot should focus on your recommendation algorithms and reporting. You will need to include the necessary user experience for users to enter resumes; otherwise, you won't have data to work with. But you shouldn't spend all of your time and resources creating a perfect user experience for candidates to enter their resumes into your system. Delighting this user will not help you demonstrate your value proposition to your Champion. In the future, if applicable, you can go back and polish the UX for all users.

Plan for Unengaged Customers

Your customer is focused on running their business. Therefore, any distraction from their core responsibilities will be set aside and given a low priority. This makes a lot of sense for their business, but it's terrible news for your pilot program. In fact, many pilot programs fail simply because they never got enough attention from the customer to get them through completion.

This might sound counterintuitive since your customer is paying you for the pilot project. How is it possible that they wouldn't engage in the pilot? **The reality is that your pilot is competing against the day-to-day activities of your customer.** The Champion might be invested in testing your

Early Adopter

solution, but she still might not be able to recruit enough people from the User Ecosystem to actively engage with your product to determine whether it is a good fit or not. I've seen this happen numerous times when a vendor spends a lot of time and effort deploying a pilot project, only to wait for weeks before anybody touches their software—or having to chase around various users to get their feedback or even login into the system.

Unfortunately, there's no easy way to solve this issue. All you can do is set clear expectations with your customer. Also, make sure you define clear objectives and instructions for your users. The more you leave them to wander around your product, the less productive they will be. Offer to host group or one-on-one training sessions. Remember that you need to do anything in your power to demonstrate value to your Champion at this stage. And the only way to get there is by having your User Ecosystem engage with your software.

> **PRO TIP:** Engaging with your users at this stage is an excellent opportunity to get direct feedback and do some high-level usability testing of your product. Understanding where your users are getting stuck or what issues they are finding will help you prioritize areas to fix during your next development iteration.

Be Ultra-Responsive

The best way to gain your Champion's trust during this co-creation phase is to be as responsive as you can. For your first ten customers, you want to be available at a moment's notice to answer questions, receive feedback, or help them with something they are struggling with. Being responsive also means fixing bugs right away and incorporating customer feedback into the software weekly or even daily.

For example, when you get feedback, don't just log it in your backlog for future analysis. That will happen once your product is more mature. For now, try to go back to your customer with a sketch the next day, and if your proposed approach fixes the problem (and it's aligned with your vision), then implement it into the software during the next development iteration. Another approach is to use the "Wizard of Oz" technique, which I'll cover later in this chapter.

Work with your team on how to become highly responsive. Remember that you are still learning at this stage, so any interaction with your customer is an opportunity to learn and improve your product.

Avoid Items That Can Delay (and Derail) Your Pilot

It is your responsibility to instill a sense of urgency in your customer about your pilot program. Remember that nothing kills the momentum of a project like a significant delay.

Early Adopter

Here are a few real-world examples I've encountered:

- In the energy industry (highly regulated), we sometimes had to wait six months to get the permits to activate our solution.

- A customer wanted to complete repairs on a new facility before deploying the pilot, delaying the project for a few months.

- The person assigned to testing our solution left the company, and we had to stop the pilot until the company hired their replacement.

- We were ready to deploy a new product when the COVID pandemic hit. Unfortunately, the customer stalled the project for one year.

It is impossible to predict all possible delays, but it's a good idea to work with your team and your Champion to anticipate any challenges you might encounter. This is another reason why having not one but ten pilot customers can help you balance the risk of one of your pilot projects stalling.

Now that you are familiar with the top customer-facing challenges you will encounter when deploying your first ten pilot customers, let's switch to some obstacles and decisions you will face within your company, including how much product to build and where *not* to cut corners.

FOUR TECHNIQUES TO MOVE FAST, BUILD LESS, AND LEARN MORE

During the Early Adopter stage, you'll need to continue moving fast, creating assumptions, running experiments, and developing your solution based on customer evidence.

So how do you move fast?

Here are four field-tested techniques that will help you deliver the value of your solution as fast as possible, with a reduced timeline, investment, and effort from your team. The techniques are:

1. Instrument your software from the very beginning.

2. Run "Wizard of Oz" experiments.

3. Leverage off-the-shelf technology.

4. Don't optimize for cost, size, performance, or scale.

Let me elaborate on each one of these techniques.

Instrument Your Software from the Very Beginning

Pilot programs offer a unique opportunity to work closely with your customer to fine-tune your product's direction and get rapid feedback on what is working and what is not. In addition to this direct customer collaboration, you must instrument your software to get an in-depth look at how your customer uses your product.

If you are not familiar with the term, *instrumenting* a piece of software means adding snippets of code that record your user's actions so you can analyze them later. By instrumenting your software, you'll gather data on how much your customer is using your product, which modules they are using the most, which user types are most engaged, where your users are getting stuck, etc.

Getting user data via instrumentation will provide you with strong evidence on whether your product is delivering value or not. Once you have the instrumentation in place, you'll be able to correlate the qualitative feedback you get by talking to your users with the quantitative information you are getting directly from the software.

For example, users might not admit they are stuck or are having issues with your software. They might tell you they love a certain functionality when in reality, they never use it. Having the information on how your customers are using your software will enable you to make data-driven decisions on what to build and what to cut.

A word of caution about instrumentation: collecting user data can feel borderline like spying. Ensure you are transparent with your customers on what data you plan to gather and what you plan to do with it. You should include this information in a privacy section as part of your pilot contract. Also, make sure you comply with any data policy from your customer and your company, as well as any government regulations that might apply.

Run "Wizard of Oz" Experiments

In a pilot program, your customers are not "paying you to learn." Instead, they are paying you to help them achieve their business outcomes. Therefore, they expect a working solution with the necessary features to address their pain in a way that is better, faster, or cheaper than what they are doing today. But this doesn't mean that you need to build your entire solution right away. As long as you meet the customer's needs, it doesn't matter *how* you do it, whether you implement it in the software or provide that value in a roundabout way. That's where "Wizard of Oz" prototypes come into play.

The term comes from the *Wizard of Oz* movie. At the end of the film (spoiler alert), Dorothy and her friends learn that the Wizard of Oz was no wizard at all. It was just a man behind a curtain playing pretend. But to the people of Oz, there was no difference between a real, all-powerful wizard and the man behind the curtain pretending to be a wizard.

You can use the same approach when delivering solutions to early adopters. In your customer's eyes, the product should be full-featured and have the necessary functionality to meet their needs. But that functionality doesn't have to be implemented as part of your technology stack on day one. Instead, your team can play Wizard of Oz and work manually, behind the scenes, to provide the necessary value to your customer. By using this technique, you'll be able to quickly add new functionality and test it with your customers before investing in the development effort to build this functionality.

There's a lot of literature on running Wizard of Oz experiments, so I won't go into detail here. But for reference, I've included a real-world example of a Wizard of Oz experiment at the end of this chapter.

When working with your first ten customers, remember that your goal is to co-create, build trust, and deliver value. Therefore, be transparent with your customers on which features are built into your product and which ones are a prototype using Wizard of Oz or any other experimentation technique.

Leverage Off-the-Shelf Technology

Early adopters care about the value you deliver regardless of how you deliver that value, but leveraging off-the-shelf technology can be a tricky proposition, especially for engineering-driven companies. The thinking goes that if you don't build as much of the solution as possible, then you won't have any differentiated intellectual property. Therefore, your product won't be worth that much. There is some truth to that, but that only applies later in the product lifecycle.

At this stage of the innovation journey, you can move the fastest by "assembling" your solution with off-the-shelf components and building the least amount possible. Focus on building any differentiated, value-providing components yourself and then use off-the-shelf technology for everything else.

This rule applies both to software and hardware. Many companies believe they need to develop their own hardware from the very beginning to provide differentiated value. But building hardware is a very time-consuming and expensive way to validate whether your solution solves your customer's needs.

For example, I've gotten creative with my teams by placing a smartphone inside an industrial enclosure and using the smartphone's sensors, screen, and operating system to run our application. We were able to mash-up this solution in just a few days and then deploy it in the customer's environment to gather data and start testing, providing value and learning right away. Of course, we could have built our own hardware to acquire the same data and provide the same value, but by leveraging off-the-shelf hardware, we were able to deliver a solution in just a few days, as opposed to months.

Technology has advanced tremendously, and it's incredible to see the variety of software and hardware components you can find on the market—whether it's single-board computers, sensors, connectivity platforms, cloud platforms, AI models, UI frameworks, you name it. Leverage anything you can from existing vendors or even from open source. Once you get enough evidence that your solution delivers on its promise, you can separate the key components you need to build and orchestrate a more robust implementation. But that happens much later.

> **PRO TIP:** Open source licenses might conflict with how your company plans to license, distribute, or commercialize your solution. To reduce risk, talk to your Legal team before incorporating any open source component into your prototypes.

Don't Optimize for Cost, Size, Performance, or Scale

Throughout your journey, you'll face a lot of pressure, both from the market and your company's leadership, to deliver solutions that maximize the company's profits. Of course, that is the right mindset when a product is in a growth stage. But when you are early in the innovation journey, your focus should be on learning and moving quickly, which means deferring cost, size, performance, or scale optimizations until you have clear customer evidence that those investments will provide a return.

Let me illustrate this rule with an example. Marcos was the CEO of a successful company delivering software and hardware automation products for the building industry. When I started coaching Marcos and his team, they were already negotiating with a Chinese contract manufacturer to develop custom hardware to deploy as part of their pilot program. He explained that their current prototype worked OK, but the hardware needed to have a smaller footprint and be cheaper to have a chance on the market. Therefore, Marcos was planning to spend a few million dollars creating a smaller, more affordable hardware device to entice customers and increase margins. I understood where Marcos was coming from. His background was managing growth-stage products, and therefore, he was executing the playbook he knew. Also, his customer insights came from talking to a few existing customers who validated his assumptions. But after probing deeper, it turned out these customers were not early adopters, so their view was biased towards growth-stage products.

I convinced Marcos to pause the manufacturing contract until the team could validate the desirability and viability of his existing prototype. After running a few experiments, Marcos' team came back with unfortunate results. All the experiments had failed, not because of cost or footprint, but because the product didn't have several key features that addressed the customer's key pain points.

The moral of the story is that, by focusing on learning and not looking to optimize for cost right away, Marcos' team was able to learn fast and save millions of dollars by canceling their manufacturing contract.

In this example, I focused on the risk of optimizing for hardware cost and size too early. But the same is true for any type of software optimization. I talk to many teams who delay their initial pilots because they are busy optimizing their software to run much faster or support millions of concurrent users. And although engineering teams might feel they are making progress towards launching a successful product, the reality is that these efforts are often wasted at this stage.

EIGHT AREAS YOU SHOULD NOT CUT CORNERS

The solution you deliver to your first ten pilot customers will still be a prototype. Prototypes don't have all the features to meet the needs of every user in the ecosystem. They are often a mash-up of custom software and off-the-shelf technologies that are not optimized for cost, performance, or scale. But this doesn't mean that your prototype will be half-baked. Your customer is paying for a functional pilot that will deliver value, so even early adopters will not put up with half-baked products.

Therefore, even though your focus is on learning and speed of delivery, you must *not* skip any of these eight critical areas:

1. Regulations

2. Stability

3. Cybersecurity

4. Safety

5. Privacy

6. Sustainability

7. Ethics

8. Standards

These areas will take time, but you shouldn't see them as time-wasters. Instead, think of them as necessary for your product to even be considered in a B2B setting. Without attention to these areas, most companies will not even entertain engaging in a pilot program with you. So think of these items as door openers and risk mitigators you must tackle early on.

Each of these areas is big and deserves a book of its own. Instead of diving deeper into each area, my goal is to showcase why they are essential for your pilot and ensure you prioritize these areas in the early versions of your product.

> **NOTE:** You must discuss these eight areas with your team as early as in the Solution Planning stage so you can start incorporating them in your working prototype. The reason I included them in the Early

> Adopter stage is that if you don't have any customers, then you should focus on building customer-facing workflows first. Focusing on ethics or regulations when you have no users can be a distraction. But, the moment you have some level of desirability, feasibility, and viability, and you have companies interested in pilot projects, you should assess with your team which of these areas are must-haves for you to close your first pilot project. I trust, now that you have this knowledge, you'll bring it up with your team early enough in the innovation journey.

Regulations

Complying with regulation means that your product doesn't break the law. It sounds easy, but complying with regulations can be much harder than it seems. For example, your product might need to comply with regulations around data, safety, and cybersecurity—or industry-specific regulations such as those in the healthcare or energy industry.

Regulations vary by industry and by geography—not to mention they change all the time. Therefore, it's essential to seek expert advice. If you are part of an established company, involve your legal and compliance teams. They need to understand your goals and roadmap to make sure you won't expose the company to any legal risks. On the other hand, if you are part of a startup or smaller company that doesn't have a compliance team, seek expert advice from third-parties or consultants.

These expert reviews will take time and money, but they are necessary to ensure your product is compliant and won't get you into legal trouble. When engaging with early adopters, don't be surprised if their procurement team asks you to demonstrate compliance with the applicable industry rules and regulations. It's a standard procedure, and you need to be prepared to meet any required rules, regulations, and even certifications.

Stability

During your pilot, delivering a stable product is a must. Nothing kills customer trust and momentum faster than a buggy, unreliable product.

Early adopters are willing to try out unproven technology to solve a burning pain, but that doesn't mean they are willing to put up with an unstable solution crashing all the time or returning incorrect results. Therefore, your product must be stable to instill confidence in your customers.

It's important not to confuse stability with scalability. These concepts are independent of each other: you can have a stable solution that doesn't scale or a large-scale solution that's not stable. **Both scalability and stability take a significant**

amount of engineering resources, so at this stage of the journey, aim for a stable solution even if it doesn't scale to large numbers of users or cannot process large amounts of data.

You don't need a product that scales at this stage. Instead, use those resources to iterate quickly on value-added features that can help you gain further evidence that your product can deliver on its promise. Once you deliver value to your first ten pilot customers, you'll be able to plan your next steps, and at that point, you can decide to invest in scaling your solution.

Cybersecurity

Cybersecurity is one of the first areas that gets pushed aside and labeled as "to figure out later." But unfortunately, later never comes, and that is why there are so many vulnerable products on the market.

Cybersecurity refers to your product's ability to deflect any intrusions and ensure no unwanted actor will harm the product, its users, and any of its data. Building secure solutions is not a one-and-done deal. Instead, it is a constant process throughout your product's lifecycle.

Your product will be as strong as the weakest of its components. I recommend using your Solution Diagram as a conversation starter with your team. Discuss how you are securing every component and what the plan is to secure any weak links.

Cybersecurity can be a door-opener or a blocker for you to win pilot projects. When negotiating a pilot project with your Champion, her procurement and IT teams will want to understand how your product tackles security. They'll scrutinize what you have implemented, how you've implemented it, and how you will respond in the event of a security breach. Your team must have clear answers to these questions; otherwise, you are not likely to get that pilot contract. I've been on both sides of this discussion, as a vendor and as a Champion. As a vendor, you need to be ready with all the answers to convince your customer that your early solution is secure. And as a Champion, I remember involving and needing the final approval of IT, Cyber and Information security, and procurement teams before moving forward with a pilot.

In short, your team needs to focus on implementing security best practices from the very beginning. Failing to do so can have big reputation and liability risks for your company, plus it will significantly affect your chances to close pilot projects.

Safety

Safety is another area that is often overlooked. Safety refers to how likely your product is to harm people or property. Safety concerns are more significant when your solution interacts with hardware because now you have a link to the physical world, and you can instill physical harm on people or property.

When I coach leaders about safety, the conversation often goes toward extreme examples, such as self-driving vehicles or drones. But safety issues can occur in more straightforward products as well. I've seen it all firsthand. I've seen industrial computers catch on fire, circuit boards explode, and workers lose their fingers to rotating machinery run by faulty software.

Depending on your industry, you might need to comply with safety regulations. In those cases, you'll need to certify your product with a third-party organization before it's deemed safe for deployment, even for a pilot. But even if your industry doesn't have those regulations, it's essential to ensure that your early solution is as safe as possible. The last thing you want is your prototype burning down a customer warehouse or triggering the fire alarm at a hospital. Companies rarely recover from such a big reputational hit.

Privacy

You must put extra emphasis on protecting the privacy of your customer and your company. The best way to approach privacy is with *transparency*. From the very beginning, make it very clear for your customer and your company what data you plan to collect, how you will use that data, and who has access to that data inside your organization. Disclosing your privacy practices is not only the right thing to do, but it's very likely something you'll need to do as part of negotiating a pilot contract.

As you deliver value to your first pilot customers, you are likely to learn new ways to leverage your customer's data to provide additional value to your customer and your company. Therefore, treat your privacy policy as experiments and test them out with each new pilot engagement. You might find that some companies are OK with your plans and some are not. Use this opportunity to learn and fine-tune your data strategy and privacy policies for the future.

Now, contractual language aside, make sure that your product delivers on your privacy promises. That means allocating time in your development lifecycle to test the areas where privacy could be compromised. I've seen situations where the privacy violations were not due to malice or lack of transparency but instead resulted from software bugs that allowed unauthorized users to access data from other users, competitors, and even your own company. Like security and safety, make sure you test out various privacy scenarios to ensure you comply with what you are promising.

Sustainability

As sustainability gets more ingrained in your customers' day-to-day operations, an increasing number of companies will look at sustainability as essential criteria for vendor selection. If your product doesn't meet your customers' sustainability requirements, you won't be considered even for an early pilot. Plain and simple.

The key areas that your customer's sustainability and corporate responsibility department will care about include:

- How energy-hungry is your solution?
- Are you powering your solution with clean energy?
- How much waste does your solution create (e.g., packaging, exhausts, end-of-life recycling)?

Creating sustainable products is usually a supply chain challenge. Therefore, as you choose your technology partners, you should evaluate them in the same way that your customers will evaluate you. For example, you should choose cloud infrastructure from companies that power their data centers with 100 percent renewables or choose your packaging from vendors who use only recycled materials.

Building a sustainable product is the right thing to do for the environment and society. But it can also be another differentiator that will open doors for your pilot and may become a baseline requirement for customers even to consider you as a vendor. So start incorporating sustainable development practices early in your product, and you'll be ahead of the game.

Ethics

I refer to product ethics as the responsibility you have to ensure your product avoids discrimination or bias, cannot be easily weaponized, and cannot be used in nefarious ways. Common examples include the disinformation engines in social media platforms or the many cases of IoT devices used to spy on people. Make sure you work with your team to understand any scenario where your product might run into ethics issues and create a plan to address it. More and more companies are placing importance on product ethics, so don't be surprised if your Champion asks you about the steps you are taking to ensure your product is as ethical as possible.

Standards

Enterprise software does not live in a vacuum. Instead, your solution will need to integrate with many other systems already in use by your customer. To ensure interoperability, your product must implement the standards that are common in your target market.

There are technology standards that go across multiple industries, such as using RESTful APIs for cloud-based solutions. But, on the other hand, there are many standards that are unique to each industry, such as CAN bus in the automotive industry or BACnet in the building industry.

The takeaway is that you need to work with industry SMEs to understand the standards of your target market. It doesn't matter if your engineering team comes up with a technologically superior approach. If you are to play in a particular industry, you need to play by that industry's rules.

Those eight areas will be present throughout your product's lifecycle, so start incorporating them early on. They require time, money, and multi-department collaboration. Therefore, make sure you seek constant support from your Advisory Board and leaders from various departments, including engineering, legal, compliance, corporate responsibility, cybersecurity, etc.

REAL-WORLD STORY

I experienced a great example of Wizard of Oz prototypes when working with a company developing enterprise software for the finance sector. During their first pilot projects, Anna, the company's product leader, learned that their product needed some very specialized reports to meet their Champion's needs. Anna was struggling with prioritizing the development of these reports since she didn't have enough engineers to build them, and at this stage, they weren't sure about what these reports should include.

Instead of building the reports without strong customer evidence, Anna decided to run an experiment by delivering the reports using a Wizard of Oz prototype. To build the reports, Anna recruited Kim, a rising star analyst from her company's customer success team. Every two weeks, Kim would manually analyze the customer data, extract some insights, and put together a report for each pilot customer.

Every two weeks, the customer would receive an email with their custom report. Anna and her team would follow up with a few of their customers to get insights on what the customer learned from the "automated" report and how they could improve it.

These reports were a big hit with Anna's customers. They had never seen such granular analysis of their data or received such actionable insights. The reports and the feedback process were instrumental for Anna's team to understand what their customers value, what data was interesting, and what data was just noise.

After a few months of creating manual reports and getting feedback from their customers, Anna's team was ready to implement an automated version of these reports as part of their core product. By leveraging a Wizard of Oz prototype, Anna and her team were able to move very fast to develop a product based on customer insights. This approach saved time but also a lot of engineering resources. Anna could have asked for a bigger team to build what they thought was needed, but that would have taken too long and would have missed the mark. Her thoughtful approach ensured they created the right solution the first time.

If you are able to deliver value to your first ten customers, congratulations! You have now completed the six stages of the B2B Innovator's Map to go from idea to your first ten customers! That's a huge accomplishment that you need to celebrate and be proud of. Now, it's time to meet with your leadership team to discuss the next stage of your journey. Good luck!

Learn More

I covered a lot of topics in this chapter, and you might feel overwhelmed with all the areas you need to cover. Don't be. You don't need to be an expert in every area. You just need to understand the basic principles of topics like cybersecurity, sustainability, standards, privacy, ethics, etc., and surround yourself with experts who can support your journey.

Here are some great books to get you started, and I've included additional resources as part of your B2B Innovator's Kit:

- *Crossing the Chasm: Marketing and Selling Disruptive Products to Mainstream Customers* by Geoffrey Moore

- *Hackable: How to Do Application Security Right* by Ted Harrington

- *Cradle to Cradle: Remaking the Way We Make Things* by Michael Braungart

- *Future Ethics* by Cennydd Bowles

Note: *For an extended list of books, the companion workbook, and additional resources, download your B2B Innovator's Kit at https://danielelizalde.com/b2b-innovators-kit.*

The Next Stage in Your Innovation Journey

DRIVING INNOVATION IS LIKE DRIVING A RACE CAR: YOUR objective is to go as fast as possible to win the race and beat your competition. You need speed, skill, grit, and patience to win the race.

You can't win a race by going full-throttle all the way. Otherwise, you'd spin out and hit a wall at the first corner. Instead, as the first corner approaches, you need to slow down and use just enough throttle to keep the momentum going. As you exit the turn, you'll start unwinding the steering wheel and then gently providing more throttle as your car gains traction. This allows you to exit the turn at maximum speed and avoid spinning out.

In innovation, investment is like the throttle of your race car. Many companies go full-throttle all the way, meaning they invest in entire development teams and big sales organizations before gaining enough traction in the market. That's why they often spin out at the first turn, and they crush their chances to win the race or even compete. The lessons you learned in this book allow you to slow down and use the right amount of investment to keep the momentum going. Once you get traction with your first ten customers, you are ready to accelerate the investment that will propel your product forward.

In this book, you used the B2B Innovator's Map to chart your way through the six stages between idea and your first ten customers. I focused on these six distinct stages because they carry most of the risk and that's where most companies fail. Stages one, two, and three of the journey focus on understanding the problem to solve, the market, and the people who experience that problem. Stages four, five, and six focus on incrementally testing and developing your solution to address that problem.

You covered a lot of ground and it's easy to feel overwhelmed. Don't be. Remember that this book is your innovation map, and you can always come back to review the specific techniques you learned. Your key takeaway is to remember that there are six stages in the B2B Innovator's Map, and each one has a distinct role in helping you reduce uncertainty and gain traction in the market.

To summarize, here are the six stages and the main takeaways from each one.

The Next Stage in Your Innovation Journey

- **Strategic Alignment:** You learned the importance of working with your leadership team to agree on the innovation direction and decide what business outcome your company wants to focus on. You also learned how to select an innovation team and your Advisory Board.

- **Market Discovery:** I showed you how to analyze various markets to look for the best opportunities around the customer business outcome you wanted to explore. You also learned how to size that market, and learned how to dive deep into the needs and pains of your Champions.

- **User Discovery:** You learned to identify your User Ecosystem and clarify their pains and opportunities where your product could deliver value across the enterprise product lifecycle.

- **Solution Planning:** I shared with you how to organize all the market and user information you collected and how to define a Solution Diagram to align your company on the potential product you could build. You also learned how to organize and test all your assumptions in an experiment roadmap.

- **Prototyping:** You learned how to evolve your solution from sketches to clickable prototypes and all the way to your working prototype. You also learned essential techniques to leverage these prototypes to test for desirability, feasibility, and viability to discover if your solution would solve your customers' pains.

- **Early Adopter:** You learned how to work closely with your first ten customers to deliver value via pilot programs. Remember, completing this stage doesn't mean you are ready for scale. It only means that you have strong customer evidence that your product can solve a pain for your target market.

So now that you have that evidence, where do you go from here?

The innovation journey continues beyond your first ten customers until you can scale your product. Completing these six stages is like driving your race car out the first turn in the track at blazing speed. Now it's time to plan for the road ahead. It's time to take the lessons you learned from providing value to your first ten customers and work with your Advisory Board on your next step. Every product and situation is different, but here are some potential areas to discuss with your team:

- Invest in technical debt to solidify your current feature set.

- Based on your learnings, plan for a new experiment and product roadmap.

- Invest in sales and marketing to start accelerating your entry into the market. You are still not going for scale, but you might be ready for your next 100 customers.

- Engage with partners to serve as potential sales channels or complement your technology stack to accelerate the growth of your product.

Thinking about all of these areas feels daunting—I know because I've been in your shoes. But don't worry. All the tools and techniques you learned throughout this book are useful beyond your first ten customers. The key to developing enterprise software that customers want to buy is to iterate between testing and building your solution constantly.

WHERE DO YOU GO FROM HERE?

Earlier in this chapter, I outlined some ideas for where your product can go. But what about you, the innovator? What should your next step be?

Now that you finished this book, there are two actions I urge you to take.

The first one is to start applying these concepts today. You gained a wealth of knowledge on minimizing uncertainty and driving innovation forward. But all this knowledge means nothing if you don't apply it. Download the companion workbook and start filling it out. If you are already in the middle of the innovation journey, use the workbook as a checklist to make sure you didn't skip any steps that might derail your progress.

You have the race car. Take it out for a test drive. Get familiar with it. I'm sure you'll run off the track or spin around a couple of times, but don't worry—that's normal. You are already one step ahead of the competition because you have a map of the innovation journey. You know what lies ahead, and you know how to tackle it.

The second action I urge you to take is to share this book with your colleagues. This might sound self-serving, but hear me out. The innovation journey can feel like a dark, winding road, and you can't navigate it alone. The more your colleagues understand the journey, its various stages, and the techniques you are implementing, the more support you'll get. You will build a shared language and a shared understanding of what it takes to drive innovation forward.

I recently talked to an innovation leader who told me that he spent half of his time educating his colleagues on how to approach innovation. It was exhausting but necessary. Fortunately, you don't have to do that. I've already done the heavy lifting by compiling all the information you'll need in this book. Share this information as a way of building alliances. Create an internal book club, or find other creative ways to bring everybody along in the journey. You'll be happy you did.

The Next Stage in Your Innovation Journey

Congratulations on making it to this point! I want to thank you again for reading this book. I hope you found it helpful in your innovation journey. I'm very excited about your path, and I look forward to seeing the impact your products will have on the world.

B2B innovation is a big topic, so if you need additional resources, just know that you'll find a lot more information on my site (danielelizalde.com), including articles, interviews, templates, courses, and more. You can also contact me via my site. I'd love to hear from you and hear about your successful innovation journey!

Keep innovating!

Daniel

Acknowledgments

This book encompasses the learnings acquired over 22 years of working in the technology industry. It's impossible to thank all of the people who have helped me, inspired me, and believed in me throughout my career. Below is a feeble attempt to recognize many of you who left a mark. Thank you for everything.

TO MY FAMILY

Thank you, Megan and Maya, for all the love, support, advice, and understanding. I love my familia so much!

A mi mamá. Gracias por todo tu apoyo, fuerza y enseñanzas. Y a mi papá. ¿Qué puedo decir? Gracias y sé que estarías muy orgulloso. A Pepe, por tantos años de amistad y hermandad.

A mi tío Fausto, por inculcarme el amor a la ingeniería desde muy temprana edad.

To Margaret and Mark Clark. Thank you for all your love and support throughout the years, especially through these tough pandemic times. This book would not exist without you.

TO MY MENTORS AND INSPIRATION

I want to thank all the mentors and thought leaders who believed in me, encouraged me, and inspired me throughout my career. Some of you I know only from your books. Others, I've been fortunate to collaborate with directly. And some others, I'm lucky enough to call my friends. The list is too long to include in a single book, so apologies to those I left out.

Rich Mironov, Alex Osterwalder, Geoffrey Moore, Steve Blank, Janna Bastow, Martin Eriksson, Adolfo Grego, Cesar Gamez, Larsh Johnson, C. Todd Lombardo, Teresa Torres, Tenday Viki, Carlos Gonzalez de Villaumbrosia, Emily Kirsch, Barry O'Reilly, David Bland, Jon Morrow, Lucian Fogoros, Dan Olsen, Bruce McCarthy, and Roman Pichler.

TO MY BOOK CONTRIBUTORS

To all the people who contributed to this book by brainstorming ideas, participating in interviews, or providing feedback along the way. Thank you! This book is much better because of you.

Acknowledgments

Rich Mironov, Miguel Morales, Mateo Fernández, Neeraj Mathur, David Sheh, Rajesh Gupta, Ellery Berk, Henrik Kenani, Julie Markham, Steve Merrick, Fabienne Hansen, Wayne Irwin, Anil Khana, Jorge Zavala, Harsha Srivatsa, Phil Hornby, Steve Portigal, Gerrard J. Lin, Fan Ding, Shannon Lucas, Andreas Rudolph, Barry O'Reilly, Carla Quant, Dan Corbin, Eddie Gotherman, Jin Zhang, Kacy Harding, Lisa O'Malley, Nancy Wang, Rohit Prabhakar, Ronnie Pettersson, Shuo Zang, Tamara Cross, Vish Pai, Rob Fitzpatrick, and the Scribe team.

About the Author

DANIEL ELIZALDE IS A PRODUCT EXECUTIVE WITH OVER 20 years of experience leveraging emerging technologies to drive product innovation in industries such as climate tech, eCommerce, manufacturing, telecommunications, automotive, and semiconductors.

Daniel has held various leadership positions, including VP, Head of IoT at Ericsson, Head of Products at Stem (AI-powered energy storage company in Silicon Valley), and Instructor at Stanford University. As a Product Innovation Coach, Daniel has trained and advised over 1,500 product professionals around the world on how to take their ideas to market. Daniel is also a mentor at Greentown Labs, the largest climate tech accelerator in the US, helping startups address some of the world's most pressing challenges. Explore his training programs, blog, newsletter, *Enterprise Product Leadership* podcast, and more at https://danielelizalde.com.

Made in United States
Troutdale, OR
05/14/2024